THE MIND ON FIRE

THE MIND ON FIRE

Blaise Pascal

Edited by James M. Houston

Introduction by Os Guinness

HODDER AND STOUGHTON

LONDON SYDNEY AUCKLAND TORONTO

Originally published under the title
THE MIND ON FIRE: AN ANTHOLOGY OF THE WRITINGS
OF BLAISE PASCAL
edited by James Houston. Published by Multnomah Press, 10209 SE
Division, Portland, OR 97266, USA. All rights reserved.

British Library Cataloguing in Publication Data

Pascal, Blaise *1623–1662*
   The mind on fire.
   1. Christian life. Spirituality
   I. Title   II. Houston, James *1921–*   III. Pascal, Blaise
   1623–1662. Pensees   IV. Pascal, Blaise *1623–1662*
   Provinciales
   248.4

   ISBN 0-340-54611-5

*Published by Hodder and Stoughton, a division of Hodder and Stoughton
Ltd, Mill Road, Dunton Green, Sevenoaks, Kent TN13 2YA. Editorial
Office: 47 Bedford Square, London WC1B 3DP.*

Printed in Great Britain by Cox & Wyman Ltd, Reading.

CONTENTS

Contents

LETTERS WRITTEN TO A PROVINCIAL BY ONE OF HIS FRIENDS

A PRAYER OF PASCAL, ASKING GOD TO USE SICKNESS IN HIS LIFE APPROPRIATELY

Contents

THE MIND ON FIRE

EDITOR'S NOTE
ABOUT BLAISE PASCAL
AND THE RELEVANCE OF HIS
CHRISTIAN WRITINGS

Many people in today's secular society believe that to become a Christian means committing intellectual suicide. They think that to accept its tenets is to join a crowd of illiterate and superstitious fools.

Pascal refutes this belief. He wrote to communicate the Christian faith to the skeptical, to the indifferent, and to the hostile. Pascal was a mathematical genius, a physicist, and a remarkable religious thinker.

HIS LIFE

Blaise Pascal (1623-1662) was born in central France, in Clermont, the son of a government official. A remarkable thinker, he has been regarded by many as the greatest of French prose writers. Because his mother died when he was only three years old, he grew up mothered by his sister Gilberte, three years his elder. Jacqueline, his younger sister by two years, was his close companion.[1]

He grew up in an age of self-evident religious faith. The skepticism of Montaigne, the rational empiricism of Descartes, and the atheism of Vanini were beginning to seduce men's minds toward the spirit of modern secularism. Although France's Catholic kings prevented Protestantism

11

from becoming a public influence in the country, powerful religious tensions still were at work. While the Jesuits sought to import a liberal casuistry, other intense religious movements of renewal were growing in importance, influenced by the spirituality of Francis de Sales, Bérulle, and Vincent de Paul. The abbot of Saint-Cyran, Jean Du Vergier de Hauranne, particularly expressed an ardent desire for spiritual renewal. He was himself influenced by the Dutch theologian Cornelius Jansen, later the Bishop of Ypres. Imprisoned for five years by the French government, Saint-Cyran died shortly after his release, but not before Pascal's father Étienne had come under the influence of two of his disciples.[2]

When Blaise was seven years old, his father left his government office in Clermont and came to Paris. It was there that his children, though taught by him personally, came under the influence of the free thinking, skeptical spirit of Montaigne, and it was there the Pascal children were exposed to a worldly and fashionable life. For a short period Blaise's father left Paris in exile, in disfavor with Cardinal Richelieu. Later he was reinstated and appointed Royal Commissioner in charge of taxes in Normandy.

Scientific studies fascinated Blaise. At the age of sixteen he presented his first mathematical treatise on the properties of the sections of a cone.[3] At the age of nineteen Blaise began working on a calculating machine designed to aid his father in the laborious task of assessing and collecting taxes. After many years of refinements, he offered his "arithmetic machine" for sale, but its prohibitive price never made it a financial success.

After an accident in 1646, Pascal's father—attended by a priest who had become an adherent of the Jansenist renewal movement—became convinced that "the Christian religion obliges us to live solely for God and to have no other object than Him." Meanwhile, Blaise's sister Jacqueline announced a clear call to enter a religious vocation. With all this family interest in religion, Blaise began to study the Bible seriously, though he continued his scientific experiments. In 1646 he reproduced the well-known experiment of Torricelli on the existence of a vacuum. Later he experimented on the measurement of air pressure on the top of the Puy de Dôme in order to demonstrate the decrease of air pressure with elevation.

Although Jacqueline was thwarted by her father from entering a convent, she was permitted to make occasional visits to the Convent of Port-Royal-des-Champs, south of Paris. Étienne died in 1651, and Blaise began to think more seriously about life after death. After Jacqueline left him to enter the convent, he threw himself once more into the worldly society of Paris. When his sister thoroughly disapproved, Blaise realized how confused he really was. On the night of 23 November 1654, while reading the seventeenth chapter of John's Gospel, he had an ecstatic experience. Mysteriously, the emptiness of his previous life became filled with the presence of God within. As the ecstasy began to fade, he quickly reached out for paper and wrote "The Memorial" (reproduced at the beginning of this anthology). He made a parchment copy which he sewed within the lining of his jacket, a practice he repeated each time he replaced his clothes during the next eight years until his death. But he told no one, not even his sister Jacqueline, what had happened to him that night.[4]

The following January he paid the first of several visits to Port-Royal. The community there sought spiritual renewal by striving to live a self-abandoned life of devotion to God in response to God's irresistible grace. Pascal found there a life as morally rigorous as previously he had sought to make intellectually vigorous. Through his contacts at Port-Royal Blaise became caught up in a controversy between the King's Confessor, Father Annat, and the leader of the Jansenist community, Antoine Arnauld. Arnauld had published two letters in support of Jansen, whose work had been condemned as heretical by Rome in 1653.

After prolonged discussion, the Sorbonne Faculty of Theology censured Arnauld in 1656. Arnauld decided to take his case to the French public and asked Pascal to help.

With two friends who supplied suitable quotations and statements, Pascal began to write anonymous letters, eighteen of which were written between January 1656 and March 1657. Five of these letters are reedited in shortened form in this anthology. They were acclaimed with great delight by the public, since they were written so lucidly and, as Voltaire claimed, established Pascal as the finest prose writer of France. Yet the author's true identity remained concealed until 1659.

Pascal attacked the whole basis of the Jesuit religious casuistry, with its moral laxity and mental reservations known as "probabilism." The Jesuit position was realistic about human nature, but ignorant about God's grace. This Pascal attacked brilliantly. In contrast, the Jansenists insisted upon the radical nature of conversion, the need for daily repentance for sin, and the irresistible grace of Jesus Christ. To Pascal, this emphasis rang true to his own experience of conversion and the new life of grace.

In his final years, Pascal began to write a Christian apologetic. In 1657 and 1658 he feverishly gathered together a large body of notes that he planned for this purpose. These were sorted into twenty-one bundles or *liasses* which are the sections (in Roman numerals in this anthology) of his *Pensées.*[5] But he was constantly interrupted by sickness, which dogged him all his short life from the age of twenty-four on. The last few years of his life he was particularly weakened, and probably in 1660 he composed his "Prayer for the Good Use of Sickness" that concludes our anthology. In 1661, a bitter conflict broke out between the authorities and Port-Royal, leading to the dissolution of the community and to the death of his sister Jacqueline. The next year, on 19 August 1662, Pascal died. His last remembered words were those of "The Memorial": "My God never leave me!"

PASCAL'S THOUGHT

After Pascal's conversion at the age of thirty-one, he records how his mind blazed with the burning conviction of being overwhelmed by light. A certitude seized him that endowed him with a new level of knowledge.[6] Now the grandeur of the human soul, in spite of the reality of human sin, gripped him with new power. For many years he had examined God merely as a series of concepts. Now he stood before God's presence and the reality of God himself, the same God who had appeared to Abraham, Isaac, and Jacob. "The God of the philosophers" Pascal now saw as a merely theoretical god, not the personal being with whom he could enjoy a lifelong relationship. It was this that now gave him "joy, joy, joy, tears of joy." There entered into Pascal's soul "certitude, heartfelt joy, and peace." He saw that man was given the gift of a new dimension of knowledge, the entry into a new level of existence.

It was during the remaining eight short years of his life that his *Pensées* were produced. Pascal clearly saw that through reason alone one could not come to understand all of reality. Knowledge cannot ascertain the whole; it can only replace the wholeness with a pretension to the whole. In fact, the whole is replaced by reduction. Pascal challenged the reductionism that he saw in the writings of men such as Montaigne. He saw there were differing levels of knowledge at infinite distances from each other. Just as the intelligence of man is infinitely distinct from matter, so man's soul is at an infinite distance from God. In the *Pensées* Pascal sees with unequivocal clarity the need for appropriate forms of knowledge. He says:

> The infinite distance between bodies and minds symbolizes the infinitely more infinite distance between minds and charity; for charity is supernatural.

> All the glory of greatness has no luster for people engaged in intellectual quests.

> The greatness of intellectuals is invisible to kings, to the rich, to captains, to all those great according to the flesh.

> The greatness of wisdom, which is nothing if not of God, is invisible to the carnal-minded and to

intellectuals. So there are three orders differing in kind.

Great geniuses have their dominion, their splendor, their greatness, their victory, their glory, and have no need of carnal greatness which has no relation to their domain. They are seen not by the eyes, but by the minds, and that is enough.

The saints likewise have their dominion, their glory, their greatness, their victory, their splendor, and have no need of carnal or intellectual greatness which has no relevance to their domain, for it neither adds to nor detracts from it. They are seen by God and the angels, not by bodies or curious minds. God suffices them.[7]

If this is so, then the fact that Jesus Christ came into this world without riches and honor, having his own glory and holiness, means that we should not stumble at his humility and patience. For he did not reign in sensual splendor, nor did he make intellectual inventions. If Christ's life was of such a different order, why then be scandalized by his lowliness? For the moral order is infinitely different from the sensual or intellectual levels of mankind. Since each is qualitatively different, each must continue to have its appropriate way of knowing.

But the misery of man is that he is lost, and he cannot find the appropriate ways of knowing simply by the use of his intellect. Indeed, Pascal was surprised to find so few in his own day actually investigating the nature of man. Perhaps it was just as well, as he saw that man was caught in dialectical tension, "a thinking reed" whose nobility lay in his intellect, and yet whose search for truth was futile and therefore whose quest for happiness was frustrated. We desire truth, Pascal argued, but we can never be sure we have attained it. We need happiness, but again we can never be sure we have reached it. So reason is sabotaged on all sides, and its foundations are uncertain. Likewise, we hanker after justice but have no true knowledge of it. Misery, then, he saw to be the key to the life of man. "Vanity of vanities" is how the writer of Ecclesiastes describes the human condition. We are wretched, yet we also see our greatness, and to see our misery is to make us most wretched.

Man with God, however, can have faith, and Pascal saw that faith sees beyond the limitations of reason. Faith can see the futility of mere philosophy, whether it be Platonist, Epicurean, or Stoic. For the Christian, faith sees and describes the human predicament as nothing else can. The Christian explanation of sin—of man's duality—takes account of man as no philosophy can. We are faced with the Christian claim and must either accept or reject it. When we see that rationalism itself is a form of self-love, indeed rebellion against God, then we have a wholly new perspective on the fallenness of man's reason. The Scripture declares two great truths: Man is fallen, but he has been redeemed.

At the center of these claims lies the further claim of Jesus Christ to be the Redeemer of mankind. It is a doctrine that explains both man's predicament and his possible redemption. It is a doctrine that harmonizes well with personal experience. For even the view of God, both hidden and revealed, reminds us constantly of our ambiguity—fallen, yet capable of redemption.

The Scriptures point to the Messiah, as did even the rabbinical writings. The Christian gospel has a long and continuous history. The prophets predicted his coming eons ago. This contrast with other religions—the historical continuity of God's action in history—impressed Pascal deeply. The New Testament is in continuity with the Old Testament promise, and affirms that Messiah has come. Jesus Christ himself made clear the hidden implications of the Old Testament. To receive him and to believe in him requires conversion, and here Pascal stops, for he clearly saw that while belief is reasonable, it is more than reasonable. Personal faith in Jesus Christ is God-given. It requires a leap, what he calls "a wager," that life will prove to be true.

After accepting the faith with our minds, we must then

take the final step of turning over our wills to God, and to discipline ourselves to build new habits. We wait and depend upon God's grace to do so. Pascal concludes with this final stage in his apologia, the need of conversion. For if unbelief is unreasonable, this does not mean that belief is simply reasonable and nothing more. If our will and imagination were turned toward God, we would see things differently from the rationalist who has never overcome self-will. Reason can pave the way, but sooner or later each individual must face the fact of the cross. To make this leap into faith can only be God-given. Otherwise we would simply justify ourselves by our own intellectual acceptance of the faith. So this is where we must humbly accept and respond to God's grace.

THE EDITING OF PASCAL'S PENSÉES

Pascal wrote down his thoughts as they came to him, postponing until later their arrangement. So when he died in 1662, his executors found the thousand odd fragments, as his nephew later wrote, "without order and with no progression of thought." Yet Pascal had known the works of other Christian apologists, notably Augustine, to whom he is particularly indebted. Pascal also wrote as an apologist. Indeed, Pascal asks us to judge his apologia, not for its original thought, but for the new way in which his thoughts were to be ordered, something which his untimely death was never to allow him to complete.

I have attempted in this anthology to both select from the *Pensées*, as well as to re-sort the materials in a way that would reconstruct the apologia along the lines indicated by Pascal himself. I am indebted to the many scholars who have argued the matter of Pascal's arrangement of the material, notably L. Lafuma and Anthony R. Pugh who have re-sorted the *Pensées* according to two seventeenth-century manuscripts.[8] The original publication of 1670 made no attempt to reconstruct the apologia along the lines indicated by Pascal himself.

Eighteenth- and even nineteenth-century editors made no attempt to discern an order closer to Pascal's original intent.

In the last generation, evidence has demonstrated that Pascal himself filed and cut up the materials into twenty-eight sections or *liasses* (indicated by Roman numerals in this anthology). The Arabic numerals to the left of the text are the list of our own selection of the *Pensées*. Since there are numerous editions and sequences by various editors, the numbers on the right side of the page represent two of the most important, namely Louis Lafuma in his edition of 1962, shown on the left of the bracket,[9] and the older edition of L. Brunschvicg of 1904, to the right of the bracket.[10]

THE SUFFERING OF PASCAL

It is appropriate to conclude this anthology with Pascal's prayer asking God to use his sickness as a blessing. All his life he struggled.[11] First, he struggled against the violence of his own inner life. That was why he was at first attracted to the Stoic attitude of Montaigne and his predecessors. He also had to struggle against the spirit of the world and of its alluring seductions for an ambitious intellectual like himself.

He further wrestled against the strong-willed trait of being a Pascal, of simultaneously loving and quarreling with his younger sister Jacqueline. The need to let go, to give up one's own self, lies deep within Pascal. Pascal had to realize, as every devotee of Christ has to learn sooner or later, that the meaning of life lies not in ourselves, but only in Christ. Growth in humility is necessary for growth in Christ. Says Jacqueline of her brother, "I saw him grow little by little so that I no longer knew him." Such is the effect of conversion by the gospel of Jesus Christ.

"Total submission to Jesus Christ and to my Director" was a new economy of the soul for Pascal, but he accepted it. In his *Pensées* he wrote: "Christian piety destroys the human ego, whereas human politeness conceals and suppresses it" (361). For Pascal, the renunciation of marriage, property, money, intellect, the smug sovereignty of one's own self-will, were all necessary. He placed himself for spiritual direction and soul-friendship with the community at Port-Royal, even though it was a community suspicious of the intellectual abilities of a genius like Pascal. It could never understand this side of Pascal; in this respect he remained alone. Without a mother, without a home, without an understanding community, he remained a lonely, suffering man. Alone, yet not alone, Pascal lived in the Scriptures, in prayer, and in self-examination before God. "Whether I am alone, or in the sight of others, in all my doings I am in the sight of God who must judge them, and to whom I have devoted them all" (931-550).

After his father died, Pascal wrote a letter in which he speaks of the essential need to see all things, whether of life or death, in the person of Jesus Christ our Mediator.

> If we look through this medium (that is Jesus Christ), we shall find nothing in ourselves but real miseries or repulsive pleasures. But if we consider all things in Jesus Christ, we shall find all is consolation, satisfaction, and edification. Let us then view death in Jesus Christ; not without Jesus Christ. Without Jesus Christ it is dreadful, it is repugnant, it is a terror of what is natural. In Jesus Christ it is altogether different. It is amiable, holy, and the joy of the believer. Everything, even death itself, is rendered sweet in Jesus Christ. It was for this he suffered. He died to sanctify death and suffering to us.

Later, probably in 1660, when Pascal had suffered a renewal of his periodic bouts of sickness, he prayed that he might "suffer like a Christian." By this he meant he would not be exempt from pain, nor be abandoned without the comforts of God's Spirit: "Oh, may I never feel pain without comfort! But may I feel pain and consolation together! . . . Sick as I am, may I glorify you in my sufferings." Pascal wished only to be filled with the glory which Christ had acquired by his sufferings and in which Christ now continues "to live with the Father and the Holy Spirit for ever and ever."

The last six months of Pascal's life were filled with intense physical suffering. He had sold everything, even his library (other than his Bible, Augustine's works,[12] and a few cherished books). He lived deeply in the Scriptures, especially in Psalm 119, which transported him in ecstasy beyond himself.

He longed to be taken to die in a hospice alongside the dying, and he longed also to celebrate the Eucharist. Both requests were denied him. In his final moments he was allowed to receive the Eucharist, and after twenty-four hours of further violent suffering, he died on the night of 19 August 1662.

Perhaps no words more eloquently express the purpose of his writings: "The heart has its reasons, that reason knows not of." As he expounds elsewhere,

> The understanding has a method of its own which is by principles and demonstrations. The heart has a method altogether different. We do not prove ourselves discerning of love by a systematic account of the causes of love; indeed, this would be ridiculous. Jesus Christ and Saint Paul have much oftener used this method of the heart, which is that of love, than that of the understanding. Because their principle purpose was not so much to inform as to inflame. Augustine does the same.

This too is why we can speak of Pascal as *The Mind on Fire*, inflamed by the love of Christ.

The text of this anthology is based upon a comparison of the French texts of L. Brunschvicg and J. Mesnard with the English texts of John Warrington and A.J. Krailsheimer in the *Pensées*. The sequence is followed in line with Anthony R. Pugh's composition of the text. For the Provincial Letters I have followed *Pascal: Oevres Complètes* (Paris: Seui, 1963) together with an edition of 1889 in English, published by Griff Farran, Okeden & Welsh, London and Sydney. Pascal's prayer is taken from *Thoughts on Religion . . . of Blaise Pascal* (Oxford and London, 1851).

I am grateful to my good friend Os Guinness, who has introduced this anthology. Like Pascal, he is a prophetic critic of our times and exemplifies the rigor of thought needed to critique whether we have Christian minds in our own society. I am also indebted to Mrs. Jean Nordlund and Mrs. Valerie Milne for their assistance in typing the manuscript.

James M. Houston

1. Roger Hazelton, *Blaise Pascal, The Genius of his Thought* (Philadelphia: Westminster Press, 1974), 16.

2. Ibid., 23.

3. Romano Guardini, *Pascal for Our Time* (New York: Herder and Herder, 1966), 24.

4. Ibid., 28-44.

5. Probably as much as 80 percent of his *Pensées* were collected together in these last years. See Philippe Sellier, *Les Pensées de Pascal* (Paris: Mercure de France, 1976), 7.

6. Hugh M. Davidson, *The Origins of Certainty, Means and Meanings in Pascal's Pensées* (Chicago: University of Chicago Press, 1979), 1-35.

7. Quoted by Hazelton, 117.

8. Anthony R. Pugh, *The Composition of Pascal's Apologia* (Toronto: University of Toronto Press, 1984).

9. This has been used by John Warrington in his translation in English, *Blaise Pascal, Pensées, Everyman's Library* (London: J. M. Dent & Sons Ltd., 1967).

10. The edition by Brunschvicg is notated by the Penguin Classics edition, trans. A. J. Krailsheimer, *Blaise Pascal: Pensées* (Harmondswotth, Middlesex, England).

11. See Guardini, 173-225.

12. Perhaps of all Christian writers, it was Augustine that influenced Pascal most of all. See P. Sellier, *Pascal et saint Augustine* (Paris: A. Colin, 1970).

CHRONOLOGY OF THE
LIFE AND TIMES OF PASCAL
(1623-1662)

LIFE AND WORK OF PASCAL	HISTORICAL EVENTS
1623 Born in Clermont-Ferrand, June 19.	Death of Pope Gregory XV. Alliance between France, Savoy, and Venice.
1627 Death of his mother.	
1631 Family moves to Paris, his father Étienne appointed to government post.	Plays of Corneille, Mairet, Balzac being shown in Paris.
1635 Blaise begins to show his precocity in science.	Formation of scientific academy by P.Mersenne, one of the first in Europe.
1640 Pascal family moves to Normandy. Étienne appointed Tax Commissioner. First publication of Pascal, "Essay on Cones."	Monetary reform in France.
1642 Pascal's first attempt to make a calculating machine (continues to 1652).	End of English Civil War. Death of French cardinal and statesman Richelieu.
1646 Pascal family becomes committed in Christian faith.	
1647 Return of Pascal to Paris for health reasons.	
1648 Blaise and his sister Jacqueline begin to relate with Port-Royal community.	Treaty of Westphalia ends Thirty Years' War. Revolt of Paris against Louis XIV, October 21.

1649	Family seeks refuge in Clermont-Ferrand.	
1651	Death of his father, September 24.	Struggle between French Parliament and monarch. Rise of Turenne.
1652	Jacqueline enters community of Port-Royal, January 4. Blaise begins notes on the *Pensées*.	Louis XIV retakes Paris, October 21.
1654	Blaise experiences his conversion to Christ, November 23.	Reconciliation between Mazarin and Cromwell.
1655	First stay at Port-Royal, and leads the duc de Roannez to Christ.	
1656	Writes the first *Provincial Letter*, January 23. The remaining 17 letters continue until 24 March 1657. He collates the *Pensées*. His niece Marguerite miraculously cured, March 24.	Partition of Poland between Sweden and Brandenburg.
1657	Composes *Elements of Geometry* for the students of Port-Royal, and the next year begins correspondence with Europe's leading mathematicians, Carcavi, Hugheus, Latouère.	French-English Alliance.
1658	Convenes a conference to explain his *Pensées* or *Apology of the Christian Religion*.	Creation of the Academy of Science in Paris.
1659	Pascal seriously ill until June 1660. Probably composed his prayer during this time (see pp. 285-92).	Marriage of Louis XIV to Marie-Therese and English Restoration. Catholic bishops censor the Jansenists.
1662	Death of Pascal, August 19.	English Act of Uniformity against Puritans.
1668	Persecution of Port-Royal.	

EDITIONS OF THE *PENSÉES*

1669-70	Committee of family and friends edit and suppress some of the *Pensées* and call it the "Port-Royal edition."
1776	New edition of Condorcet to include all *pensées* and reassemble them more logically.
1842	Discovery of two texts in the library of the Sorbonne 73 leads to edition of Faugere's text. Many other editions follow in 1873, 1879, 1896-1897.
1897	Leon Brunschvicq profits from all previous editions with his standard one, dividing the *Pensées* into fourteen subdivisions.
1952	Louis Lafuma adds further notes of Pascal to his edition of the *Pensées*, published in English, 1960.
1980	Research of Anthony R. Pugh, to revise *The Composition of Pascal's Apologia*, University of Toronto Press, 1984.

INTRODUCTION

As typical modern people, most of us are prone to the curse of "homo-up-to-datum," Daniel Boorstin's apt term for the illusion that the closer we are to instant total information, the nearer we are to wisdom. Of its many consequences, one of the more fatuous is that we seem to know everything about the last twenty-four hours but next to nothing about the last twenty-four years, let alone the last twenty-four centuries.

This myopia is part and parcel of our "last men" culture, for as Nietzsche foresaw in Thus Spake Zarathustra, most people are incapable of responding to the "death of God" by becoming heroic overcomers or "supermen." Losing touch with transcendence, they would eventually lose even the capacity to despise themselves, and end by confusing not only heaven with happiness but happiness with health.

Nietzsche's description is almost a parody of the age of joggers and dieters in which we live. Health has replaced both heaven and ethics. Athleticism is the new form of asceticism. Positive thinking is prized above reflection and meditation. Human experience with all its rich, tragic, and ironic complexities is scaled down to the glow of physical well-being. And self-knowledge and self-mastery are promised us through dieting and exercise. "One has one's little pleasure for the day and one's little pleasure for the night," Nietzsche commented, "but one has a regard for health. 'We have invented happiness,' say the last men, and they blink."

In short, a sickness of our age is that we have fit bodies but flaccid minds and vacant souls. So, like a drowsy napper who falls off to sleep after a meal and is reluctant to rouse himself to answer the telephone, we find ourselves disinclined to heed the challenge to rise above our age.

For those who do desire to rise above their times or stand outside their cultures, there are three sure ways. In ascending order, they are travel, history, and direct knowledge of God—and there are few lives and testimonies which are more help with the two deepest of these than that of Blaise Pascal.

Like Nietzsche, Pascal lived a life of lonely intellectual daring, dying young and enduring constant physical pain. Like Nietzsche, Pascal was aware of the nausea of the "abyss," though he called it "infinity" and termed its deeper consequence "vanity" rather than "weightlessness."

But there the similarities end. Nietzsche proclaimed himself the antichrist and climbed the high mountain to herald the Superman and "see the abyss but with pride." Pascal, by contrast, used the pseudonym "Louis de Montalte" (Louis of the Mountain), but was more conscious of the "high mountain" as the place where Satan tempted Jesus and viewed himself, both in heart and pen, as Christ's champion and a "friend of truth." For Nietzsche, it was the profundity of God's dying and being nothing which reduced man without God to weightlessness. For Pascal, it was the profundity of God's living and being everything that reduces man without God to vanity.

Pascal, then, I have found second only to Augustine as a hero-saint whose life is an inspiration and challenge as well as a drastic antidote to late twentieth-century discipleship.

But what has been the secret of Pascal's inspiration? For me at least, it does not lie in the superlatives that precede him. It is true that as a mathematical genius, inventor, and father of the modern computer he is one of the greatest human thinkers of all time. It is true that as a contemporary peer and confidant of such Enlightenment leaders as

Descartes and Queen Christina of Sweden, he was a truly Renaissance thinker, well-versed in mathematics, physics, philosophy, and theology. It is true that he was one of the greatest prose stylists in the French language, who wrote what French writers such as Voltaire have hailed as the greatest masterpiece in French prose.

But to most of us, these are accomplishments that can be hailed but don't much help us. They are so far beyond us that any thought of emulation leads to a moment of conceit and a lifetime of despair. Fortunately, Pascal's real inspiration lies elsewhere. In many ways, his achievements did not come easily. They were against the grain, both of his character and his times. But what lit and fanned into a blaze the deep potential of his character and gifts was something open to us all—he came to know God so deeply that he became a man consumed by divine fire.

In short, Pascal's witness across the centuries is that of a brief intense flame-burst of a life which warms our hearts, rekindles our faith, and showers a thousand sparks of truth into the darkened thinking of our times.

Let me set out some of the reasons why I have found the life and writings of Blaise Pascal to be so instructive, and why I believe they deserve a far greater audience in Christian circles today. But first, a warning: Pascal is a hero-saint, but a forbidding one. Just as the disciples followed Jesus but their faithfulness turned to fear as they saw the determination of his face set toward Jerusalem, so—for better or worse—there are elements in the story of Pascal that draw us closer, but never too close. We admire him, but sometimes only distantly and sometimes not at all.

Pascal's genius has a human side that offsets the superhuman. He loved boyish pranks. Like many of us, he was unconscionably bad at letter writing and, like some of us, he was for a while inordinately fond of fast (carriage) driving. He took great pride in devising Paris's first omnibus, and therefore its first public transport system.

But all these things, along with his deep love for his family and his devotion to poor people, are offset at times by the path on which God led him and some of the practices he chose along the way. I, for one, would choose neither his cup of pain nor his early death at the age of thirty-eight. Nor will most of us agree with the forms and lengths taken by his ascetic devotion. Choosing to remove all the tapestries from his room and to give up all sauces, ragouts, fruit, and anything that would excite his appetite is one thing. But to rebuke his sister for caressing her children and to literally "give up" his friends, or see them only if he were wearing a steel belt studded with sharp points, is quite another. Most modern readers of this book will lack any practical concept of the "mortification of the flesh," but if we recover it, our theological bent would be toward the "inner asceticism" that flowed from the Reformation rather then the external asceticism which preceded it.

Pascal, then, is about as far as it is possible to get from today's "born again celebrity" in whose glow we all glow and go on unchanged. His life and thought present a palpable reality—stubbornly, painfully, and gloriously real. They have the effect of surprising us and calling us into question at profound levels within ourselves.

It has been my privilege to read Pascal almost every year for nearly thirty years, and there are four reasons why I keep on coming back with never a thought of staleness.

First, *Pascal is to be admired and followed as a thinking believer for whom worship is primary.* Much has been made of his deep piety and the practices he used. His asceticism was performed in secret, and so also was his prayer, Bible reading, and almsgiving. According to his family, he literally knew the Bible by heart.

But what sets Pascal apart is the secret behind the piety and the practices, as set out in "The Memorial" of "the night of fire," included at the beginning of this collection. On the evening of Monday, 23 November 1654, when he was thirty-one years old and had just experienced a close brush with death in a driving accident, he had a profound encounter with God which changed the course of his life. Lasting from 10:30 P.M. until 12:30 A.M., the experience strained and

exhausted language and he could only title it in one word:
Fire. But the experience was so precious and pivotal to him
that he sewed the parchment record of it into the lining of
his doublet—and for his remaining eight years took the
trouble to sew it into every new doublet he bought.

This experience is sometimes called Pascal's "second
conversion," following the first in Rouen in 1646 when he
was twenty-four. But clearly it was the moment when he was
set ablaze by the divine fire which consumed him for the last
years of his life.

Can we understand fully what Pascal experienced? Should
we expect to duplicate it exactly in our own lives?
Emphatically not. But dare we survey the ice-cold minds of
countless thinking Christians today and not yearn for some
discernible fear of the Lord? Some working knowledge of the
spiritual dimensions of intellectual warfare? Some
irrepressible passion that betrays the fact of a direct,
immediate, and unquestionable experience of God? In an age
when attitudes to knowledge are strung out between
technicians and fanatics, between knowledge-eunuchs and
knowledge-hustlers, the distinctive Christian mind—sharp,
objective, and critical, but committed and worshiping—is all
too rare.

Second, *Pascal is to be admired and followed for the lonely
courage of his life work.* For one thing, we cannot fail to be
struck by all he might have been and had. Love of
friendships, culture, pleasures, and all the privileges of an
affluent life were Pascal's for the taking, as well as the
scintillating contacts and dazzling prospects opened up by his
genius and renown—not to speak of the offer of the hand of a
young lady said to be "the best in the kingdom by wealth,
birth, and person." To have such gifts, friends, and
opportunities in the age of France's "Sun King" (Louis XIV)
presented a golden vista from which few would have turned
aside. But, like Francis of Assisi earlier, Pascal did, and with
joy.

In addition, when Pascal switched from his mathematics to
the general defense of the faith and of Port-Royal, his own

special community in particular, he turned both from the fashionable to the ridiculed and the successful to the failed. Pascal's defense of the Jansenists in the *Provincial Letters* was brilliantly skillful and highly effective in swaying public opinion. But after two grueling years, he lost the battle. The combination of pope, king, and Jesuits was too strong. The letters were proscribed, one translation burnt publicly, there was a warrant for his arrest, and even his beloved Port-Royal des Champs was to be torn down stone by stone and the cemetery dug up, under orders from Louis XIV.

As they were later with Isaac Newton when he turned to theology from physics, many skeptics were ready with their scorn. "My friend," Voltaire scoffed to Condorcet, "never weary saying that since the [driving] accident on the Neuilly Bridge, Pascal's brain was damaged!"

Pascal's lonely courage can be seen above all in his long battle with sickness and the growing awareness of his early death. Desperately ill as a baby and sickly as a child, Pascal fought ill-health all his life. "He sometimes told us," his sister Gilberte recorded, "that since the age of eighteen he has not passed a single day without pain." His own glad obedience to the will of God shines out through his "Prayer Asking God to Use Sickness in His Life Appropriately," included at the end of this collection. But the poignancy of Pascal's courage and its temptations is captured by Gilberte's comment: "God, who had given him the requisite intelligence for such a grand accomplishment, did not give him sufficient health to bring it to completion."

Ours is a generation for which knowledge is a key to power, education a passport to wealth and fulfillment, and Christian thinking and scholarship are often chameleon-like in their adaptation to their surroundings. Pascal's life stands across our pilgrimage as an unvarnished witness to courage, vocation, and a higher possibility for us all.

Third, *Pascal is to be admired and followed for the boldness and balance of his thinking.* When we read Pascal, we find that not only are his own ideas profound and fresh, they have an uncanny power to provoke within us further ideas and yet more connections. The effect is to destroy old ruts and dismantle dusty patterns until our minds capture something of the fertile intensity of his own.

What must it have been like to live with such a laser beam of a mind or to work under such a torrent of thoughts and insights? For me, two features of his thinking stand out. One is the originality of his individual points (such as his brilliant descriptions of human "diversion" and his pre-sociological analysis of the impact of society on truth). The other is the panoramic scope of his vision of Christian truth and in particular the daring, high-wire balance of his statements of it.

Intellectual projects today are like cottages, not cathedrals. In their small coziness they make up in safety what they lack in grandeur. Pascal, by contrast, despite knowing that his master-building days were numbered, displays in both his sketched designs and the little work he does complete a rare affinity not only with the master-builders of Lincoln, Salisbury, and Chartres but with their counterparts in ideas such as Augustine.

That is not to say that Pascal was a system-builder on the order of an Aristotle and an Aquinas. For him, human thought-systems are but one more diversion from the truth. Skepticism was one of his favorite tools and the real questions he confronted were not abstract or theoretical but existential and concrete. Born of direct knowledge of his own dilemmas, his insight into the human heart squarely confronts the elemental predicament of all human existence.

Pascal's distinctive flair for balance is also rare today. Doubtless it was entirely his own, though it may, in part, have been developed against the backdrop of false alternatives on offer in his day. It must have seemed his fate always to be caught in the middle—between the orthodox and the skeptics, between the Catholics and the Protestants, between the king and his Gallican supporters and the pope and his ultra-montanists, between the Jesuits and the Libertines, between Montaigne and Epictetus, between the convent and the saloon, and between the chapel and the laboratory.

Pascal's response to standing between the opposing extremes is not a cowardly truce or mere splitting of the differences. Exploiting such tensions to the fullest, he sets out human existence itself in terms of its even deeper tensions—for example, human beings, who are neither angel nor beast, are caught between the finite and the infinite, between misery and grandeur, between reason and the heart, between reason and authority.

For Pascal, these dualisms are not ultimate, but they are the truth of a fallen world, and he uses them brilliantly to fashion a technique sometimes called the "dialectic of the contradictions." Repeatedly he demolishes arguments by setting them out in terms of polar opposites which cancel each other out when their logic is pressed to the end. Then suddenly, he shows that the contradictions can be reconciled only by introducing a third truth which contains the half truths of the faulty extremes. The gospel alone, for example, explains both man's wretchedness and his grandeur. This third truth—Christian truth—is not a synthesis born of the faults of the thesis and the antithesis. Rather it precedes and underlies the other positions, whose deficiencies grow directly from their ignorance or rejection of its full truth.

Thus dualism means that human beings are "caught" in predicament rather then capable of their own salvation. But to Pascal, their "caughtness" does not, like existentialist views of "throwness" in the twentieth century, lead toward the absurd. It becomes a jolt beyond reason and human self-sufficiency that opens up the searching sinner to look beyond himself to God.

Lastly, *Pascal is to be admired and followed for his supreme dedication to championing God and his truth.* Knowing God so deeply, his deep desire is to make him known, and the result is his dedicated commitment to apologetics, or the art of Christian persuasion.

Christian apologetics is in crisis today. Cut loose from its missionary and evangelistic setting, it has become caught between the opposing tendencies of a broad conservative movement ("Don't persuade, proclaim!") and a broad liberal movement ("Don't debate, dialogue!"). In the process, apologetics has been either widely misunderstood (as an abject apology) or narrowly defined (in a purely defensive role) and critically constricted (to certain types of argument and certain levels of educational development). Its concern and capacity to persuade real people has almost been lost.

No one seeking to recover the purpose and power of apologetics should bypass Pascal. Not only is he refreshingly different from the ineffectual approaches that passed for apologetics in his day as in ours, but he is one of the most brilliant persuaders in human history. God's existence was far too important to be left to the unconvincing proofs, convoluted reasonings, and specious arguments of theologians and philosophers. It called for a new approach shaped by the character of the goal (persuasion, or "mind-opening") as well as the nature of the instrument (the unbelieving, or closed mind).

Several features of Pascal's apologetics are worthy of note, quite apart from his actual arguments and his celebrated new style. In the first place, his sense of humility is remarkable and pertinent to all his persuasion. Apologetics, like philosophy, can be traced back to early "agonistic" contests ("mind-wrestling competitions"), and too many apologists display an egotistic bent, the constant "striving to win" that C.S. Lewis confessed in himself.

Pascal, by contrast, became unusually humble in this regard, although his precociousness as a boy left him with a natural arrogance that he knew was his besetting sin. He refused always to have his portrait painted, or to have an epitaph on his tombstone and, to the surprise of his friends, he showed (in his sister's words) "no passion for reputation" or cashing in on his mathematical brilliance. Pascal was clutching in his hands when he died a piece of paper he had often been seen reading. It read, in part: "It is unjust that anyone should attach himself to me, even though with pleasure and voluntarily. I would disappoint anyone in whom I caused such a desire to be born, and I do not have what would satisfy them. Am I not ready to die? Thus the object of their attachment will die."

But this humility, which was in sharp contrast to his contemporary, Descartes, was more than a virtue. It shaped his apologetics practically. Like Søren Kierkegaard later, Pascal knew well that the sinner's main business was not with him but with God. So, as apologist, he must keep out of the way as far as possible, acting (in the "brooding Dane's" terms) as a midwife or a theater prompter rather than as an obtruding protagonist. Hence the deliberate indirection of both their arguments. Otherwise, championing the truth is too easily debased into conquering with truth.

Another defining feature of Pascal's apologetics is his courageous commitment to it as a strategic project. People often forget the *Pensées* are incomplete; they are only the architect's sketches for his *Apology for the Christian Religion*, a monumental defense of the Christian faith that is tantalizingly unfinished. First conceived for "eight strong minds of Poitou who did not believe in God," they were sketched out in broad outline and then jotted down at white hot speed after being composed entirely—like Aleksandr Solzhenitsyn's books in the labor camps—in the mind.

So all we have is fragments, tied together in various bundles, whose final form we can only guess. Conceivably, if he had not been ill, Pascal would have written nothing until the whole work was complete, so the *pensées* we have are "bits and pieces" recorded in the teeth of enervating sickness and impending death. Again, Pascal's daring is unmistakable: His *Apology* was both soaring and compelling *by faith*.

Critics sometimes say that Pascal's arguments convince nobody today. They forget that thousands more are attracted and convinced by Pascal's "bits and pieces" today than when the *Pensées* were first published—far more, in fact, than are ever drawn to traditional proofs. But more importantly, they forget that while Pascal has won an almost universal appeal, he did not believe in timeless proofs but in "opening-up" persuasive arguments fashioned for particular people, times, and places. It is up to us today to rediscover his "foolmaking" tradition and reapply it in the service of the same God of

Abraham, Isaac, and Jacob—emphatically "not of the philosophers or of the learned," but He Who Is. In a word, the God of fire.

Once, when Winston Churchill was staying with friends in the south of France, he sat in a chill evening and stared into the fireplace. Pine logs were spitting and hissing as they burned. Then his familiar voice growled: "I know why logs spit. I know what it is to be consumed."

Men and women consume and are consumed by many things, some which only shrink and debase them. In the great person and the great cause, whatever consumes them may become a magnificent obsession and a heroic destiny. But with Pascal, as with the greatest of Christ's saints, we see the ultimate—a human being ablaze with the glory of God as if consumed with divine fire. Of course, we are only to follow Pascal in so far as he followed Christ. But to do just that is sooner or later to reach the place where our shoes must come off, for we ourselves are on holy ground.

Os Guinness

PASCAL'S TESTIMONY OF HIS CONVERSION

Memory is required for all actions of reason. (651-369)

THE MEMORIAL

[On a piece of parchment Pascal recorded the decisive experience of 1654 when he was converted. This testimony was found sewn into his clothing after his death. It appears that he carried it with him at all times.]

Year of Grace 1654

Monday 23 November, feast of St. Clement, Pope and Martyr, and of others in the Martyrology.

Eve of St. Crysogonus, martyr and others.

From about half past ten at night to about half an hour after midnight,

FIRE

"God of Abraham, God of Isaac, God of Jacob" (Exodus 3:6), not of philosophers and scholars.

Certitude, heartfelt joy, peace.

God of Jesus Christ.

God of Jesus Christ.

"My God and Your God" (John 20:17).

"Your God shall be my God" (Ruth 1:16).

The world forgotten, everything except God.

He can only be found by the ways that have been taught in the Gospels.

Greatness of the human soul.

"O righteous Father, the world has not known You, but I have known You" (John 17:25).

Joy, Joy, Joy, tears of joy.

I have separated myself from him.

"They have forsaken me, the spring of living water" (Jeremiah 2:13).

"My God, will you leave me?" (cf. Matthew 27:46).

Let me not be cut off from him for ever!

"Now this is eternal life: that they may know you, the only true God, and Jesus Christ, whom you have sent" (John 17:3).

Jesus Christ.

Jesus Christ.

I am separated from him; for I have shunned him, denied him, crucified him.

May I never be separated from him.

He can only be kept by the ways taught in the gospel.

Complete and sweet renunciation.

Total submission to Jesus Christ and to my director.

Everlasting joy in return for one day's striving upon earth.

"I will not neglect your Word" (Psalm 119:16). Amen. (913-29, 61)

THE *PENSÉES*

REARRANGED AND SELECTED AS A CHRISTIAN APOLOGETIC

I
INTRODUCTION

1. Before we examine the evidence of the truth of Christianity, I need to point out an inconsistency of those who are careless about the truth. Yet it is vital to them, for it intimately affects their lives. Of all their miscalculations, this is what most blatantly shows up their blind folly. It is this: This present life is momentary, but the state of death is eternal. How terribly important it is, then, to live in the light of the eternal, since it ultimately affects all that we do or think! Since nothing is more obvious than this observation, how absurd it is to behave differently.

Seen from this angle, how absurd it is for people to go through life without regard for their final destiny. Instead, they are led as they feel inclined and as they indulge themselves, unreflective and careless, as though they could wipe out eternity and enjoy some passing happiness merely by repressing their thoughts. Yet death is real, for it threatens us at every moment of time, while eternity is also real, and is in fact a threat of ultimate destruction and misery.

This creates the prospect of terrible consequences; indeed, it is the prospect of eternal damnation. Yet people do not even bother to find out if eternity is merely an old wives' tale. Though this stares them in the face, they do not even trouble to find out if the arguments for it are valid. They have no idea whether they should or should not refuse to face up to this question. What an appalling way to behave! (12-195)

2. How difficult it is to submit to someone else's opinion without being preoccupied about having to do so! It is natural for us to react contrarily; I think something is ugly when you think it is beautiful. That is to say, to think just the opposite of what you want me to think. Perhaps then, it is better to say nothing at all, so that someone else can think more objectively for himself and in the light of his own appropriate context. Then at least you have not interfered, unless your very silence can also be interpreted, or your very gesture, or tone of voice, can also be seen as a form of personal interference. How very difficult it is not to upset someone else's judgment; or to express this in another way, how rare it is for personal opinion to be seen firmly and consistently! (1-105)

3. Generally speaking, we are more firmly convinced by reasons that we have discovered for ourselves, than by those which are given to us by others. (6-10)

4. Whenever we want to be helpful in convincing someone that he is wrong, and so correct him, we also have to see things from his point of view. For perhaps he is right as he sees it, but he may also need to see things from a differing point of view. Perhaps it is in the nature of things that we humans never can see things from every possible angle, and so we cannot see things completely. But this should not upset us, if we realize that this lies behind all wise correction. At the same time, from one's own point of view, sense perception can be valid. (5-9)

5. We must not lose sight of the fact that we think automatically like machines, as well as doing so intelligently. That is why proving things rationally is not the only faculty we have. Indeed, how little we really do "prove." For proofs only convince the mind. But habits provide us with more effective and widespread proofs, modifying the mind, without our ever being conscious of it. For example, how can we "prove" that we shall die, or that there will be a tomorrow?

Yet what could be more obvious? It is habit that really tends
to convince us, and indeed, it makes us either Christians, or
even Turks, or pagans, or merchants, soldiers, or anything
else! In all of these, we have to act upon some faith that lies
beyond where "bare proof" will take us, although the exercise
of faith is more consciously done by Christians. So we have
to rely upon faith when the mind is convinced of the
direction in which truth lies, or to influence the mind when
truth seems to elude us. We would be overdoing things if we
insisted upon having proofs for everything we did, all the
time.

Habit, therefore, is a simpler expression of faith, which is
unforced, uncontrived, unargued, while it predisposes us to
believe, and to so favor our beliefs, that our souls naturally
acquiesce. There is something wrong with us if we have to be
convinced all the time. Instead, we need to balance specific
convictions with a habitual attitude of acceptance. As the
psalmist expresses it, "Incline my heart to your testimony, O
God" (Psalm 119:36). In contrast, reason deliberates more
slowly as it views alternatives. So it can also go to sleep, or
wander absentmindedly, when its principles are not being
applied. But feeling does not act like this. For it acts more
spontaneously, and always is ready to act. So we ought to
trust our feelings, for without doing so our faith will vacillate.
(7-252)

6. In what I am writing, let no one think I am saying
anything new. It is only the arrangement of my material that
may be new. For it is like a game of tennis, where we both
play with the same ball, but one of us uses it to better
advantage. So I would like it to be said that I am simply
using well-worn words in a new framework. For when
familiar thoughts are rearranged, they simply present a
different way of communicating the truth. So too, we can use
our words. (4-22)

PART ONE

THE MISERY OF MAN WITHOUT GOD

II
Man's Natural Condition

7. There is nothing that we can see on earth which does not either show the wretchedness of man or the mercy of God. One either sees the powerlessness of man without God, or the strength of man with God. (43-562)

8. Man's condition is one of inconsistency, of boredom, and of anxiety. (61-127)

9. Man's sensitivity to trivia, and his insensitivity to matters of major importance, reveal he has a strange disorder. (20-198)

10. Those who have known and spoken most effectively about man's misery are Solomon and Job. The one is the happiest of men, the other the most miserable. One knows by experience the vanity of pleasure, and the other knows the reality of suffering. (403-174)

11. The book of Ecclesiastes shows how man without God is completely ignorant and inescapably miserable. For anyone is unhappy whose will is caught in futility. He wants to be happy and to be assured of some conviction, and yet he is

both incapable of knowing as well as of desiring to know. He cannot even doubt. (75-389)

12. People despise Christian faith. They hate it and are afraid that it may be true. The solution for this is to show them, first of all, that it is not unreasonable, that it is worthy of reverence and respect. Then show that it is winsome, making good men desire that it were true. Then show them that it really is true. It is worthy of reverence because it really understands the human condition. It is also attractive because it promises true goodness. (12-187)

13. Man is vain to pay so much attention to things which do not really matter. These are the opinions that have to be refuted. People are still vain even when their opinions are sound, because they do not see the truth when it is there, but assume things to be true when they are not. The result is that their opinions are always completely wrong and unsound. (93-328)

14. That the vanity of the world is so obvious and yet so little recognized by people is surely an amazing thing. Yet they find it odd to be told that it is foolish to seek greatness. Surely that is most remarkable. (16-161)

15. Vanity is illustrated in the cause and effect of love, as in the case of Cleopatra. (46-163)

16. To fully understand human vanity one has only to consider the causes and effects of love. The cause may be so trivial that one can scarcely recognize it, and yet it may shake an empire to its foundations, upset princes, armies, even the whole world. It's a case of Cleopatra's nose. Had it been shorter, the whole face of the earth might have been different. (413-162)

17. What vanity is painting! It wins applause merely by representing things, while the originals are not even admired. (40-134)

18. Men are completely absorbed in pursuing self-interest. But they cannot justify their claim to it, because they have nothing but human imagination and no strength to make its possession certain. It is the same thing with knowledge, which illness can remove. So we are equally incapable of having both truth and what is good. (23-436)

19. Those who indulge in perversion tell those who are living normal lives that it is *they* who are deviating from what is natural. They think they are following a natural life themselves. They are like people on a ship who think it is those on shore who are moving away. Language is relative everywhere. But we need a fixed point by which to judge it. So the harbor is that fixed point for those who are moving aboard ship. But in morality, where are we going to find a harbor? (697-383)

20. In time of sorrow, physical science will not console me for my ignorance of morality. But a knowledge of morality will always console me for being deficient in the knowledge of physical science. (23-67)

21. Imagination is the dominant faculty in man. It is the mistress of error and falsehood, all the more so for not being evident as such an impostor. For if she were consistently false, then this would itself be an infallible criteria for what is truth. But being most often deceptive, she gives no consistent sign of her nature, and so confuses us with the same character upon what is true and what is false.

I am not speaking of fools, but of the wisest men. For it is among them that imagination carries the greatest power of conviction. In vain does reason protest; it cannot assess things at their true value.

This haughty faculty, the enemy of reason, whom she likes to dominate and rule in order to show what it can accomplish everywhere, has established in man a second nature. Imagination possesses the minds of those who are both happy and unhappy, healthy and sick, rich and poor. It makes people believe in, or doubt, or even deny reason. It suspends control of the senses by making them *feel*. It has both its fools and its wise. Nothing more frustrates us than to see how it brings satisfaction to its clients with more completeness than anything reason can offer. So people gifted with a lively imagination are much more self-satisfied than prudent men can reasonably be. Such look haughtily at others, arguing boldly and confidently, while others are more fearful and diffident; so the former's cheerful look often gives them advantage in the minds of an audience. With such self-esteem do these imagine themselves to be wise before the minds of others that have the same stamp. Of course, imagination cannot turn fools into wise men, but at least it can make them happy and competitive with reason, which can only make them feel wretched. One covers them with glory, the other with shame.

How are reputations manufactured? Who is it that gives respect and veneration to people, or books, or laws, or to the great, if it is not this faculty of the imagination? How inadequate are all the riches of the world without its cooperation!

Do you really think this judge, whose venerable age demands the respect of society, is governed purely by a noble reason, or that he decides a case on its true merits without any regard to those trivia which affect only the imagination of the feeble-minded? Look at him as he goes religiously to church to listen to a sermon, strengthening the purpose of his own reason with the ardor of his charity. There he is, ready to listen as an example to the rest of us. Suppose the preacher appears, however, and it happens that he is afflicted with a hoarse voice and he looks odd, badly shaved by his barber and perhaps unwashed. I will bet you that the judge will not keep his solemn demeanor in spite of whatever wonderful truths the preacher may be proclaiming.

Or suppose the greatest philosopher in the world were to find himself on a plank hanging over a precipice. Do you not think that even though his reason tells him he is safe, that his imagination will not get the better of him? Many cannot even bear the thought without breaking into a cold sweat. So I do not propose to go on enumerating all the effects of imagination. For everyone knows that the sight of cats or rats, or crushing a piece of coal, may be enough to unhinge people's reason. Even the tone of voice can affect the wisest, or change the mere succession of words into a powerful poem. Love or hate alter the course of justice. Do you not think that an advocate who has been well paid in advance will find his client's cause all the more just? See how his bold handling of the case appears all the more convincing to the judges who are taken in by mere appearances! How absurd the extent to which reason can be tossed hither and thither by every wind that blows.

There is scarcely an action of men which is not moved to some degree by the stimulus of the imagination. Reason is compelled to give ground, for the wisest of men accepts as his principles those which the imagination has had the nerve to introduce.

Indeed, anyone choosing to be guided only by reason would plainly be regarded as a madman. Having made his choice, he would be forced to work all day for rewards which are admittedly of the imagination. When he had been refreshed by sleep after all the efforts of reason, he would have to leap out of bed at once in order to continue the pursuit of fantasies and submit to the impressions that this mistress has over the world. Yet while it is one of the major sources of error, it is not the only one. For while man is quite right to seek an alliance between these two powers, the peace that comes from the imagination gives it a great advantage. But in war it is much more dominant. While reason will never entirely succeed in overcoming the power of the imagination, the reverse is quite common.

Our judges are well aware of the secret power of the imagination. Their red robes, the ermine fur in which they clothe themselves, looking like furry cats, the courts in which they sit, the decor of the *fleurs de lis*—all this impressive paraphernalia has been considered most necessary. Or again, if doctors do not have their cassocks and mules, with their robes and hats four times too large, they would never have fooled people who cannot resist such an impressive display. If the judges exercised true justice, and the doctors the true art of healing, there would be no need for square hats! Instead, the majesty of their science would be sufficiently imposing in itself. But since their science is purely fictitious, they have to deck themselves out with these vain ornaments in order to incite the imagination. This is how they win respect. Only soldiers do not need to disguise themselves for the part they play. For they establish themselves by force, while the rest have to give themselves airs.

So it is also with our kings, who have not looked for such disguises. They don't need to dress up in extraordinary clothes to make themselves look like monarchs. Instead they are escorted by guards and archers. The armed forces are their arms and strength. Trumpets and drums march ahead of them, while legions of soldiers surround them so that the boldest among us tremble in their presence. They don't just possess clothes, they have naked power. So one would need to have a clear head indeed to see the Turkish Sultan looking like any other man when he is dressed magnificently, standing in his splendid palace compound and surrounded by forty thousand body guards. Thus we can never look at a judge in cap and gown without forming a flattering opinion of his ability.

Imagination thus dominates everything. It creates beauty, justice, and happiness, which are all that matter in the world. I should be glad to see that Italian book which is known to me by name and which is worth a whole library: *Concerning the Royal Opinion of the World.* I approve of what it is saying without having to read it, except for anything bad that it may contain.

Such are the effects, more or less, of the deceitful faculty which seems to have been bestowed upon us deliberately to foster such necessary error. But there are also many other sources of error.

Bygone impressions are not the only ones that are capable of misleading us. The charm of novelty has the same power. So we have all the quarrels between men who blame themselves for either being taken in by the false impressions of childhood, or of running madly after new ones. Who keeps a middle way? Let him come forward and show it. For there is no principle, natural though it may be to us from infancy onwards, which cannot be dismissed as a false impression, as a result either of education or of the senses.

"Because," someone will say, "you have believed from childhood that a box was empty when you saw nothing in it and so you believed that the vacuum was possible. It's only an illusion fostered upon the senses by habit, which science must correct." Others will say: "When they told you at school that there was no such thing as a vacuum, they perverted your common sense which understood so clearly beforehand that there was." So your belief has to be corrected by returning to its original impression. Who then has deceived you, the senses or your education?

Another source of error is sickness. It will distort our judgment and our senses. So if serious illnesses alter them significantly, I have no doubt that minor ailments will do so proportionately.

Moreover, self-interest is a wonderful instrument for closing our eyes to realities in the most pleasant manner. The most just man on earth is not allowed to sit in judgment on his own situation. I know some who, in order to avoid falling for this self-interest, have gone to the opposite extreme of injustice. The surest means of losing a perfectly sound case is to submit it to those who are one's near relatives.

Justice and truth are two points which are so delicate that our instruments are too blunt to be used upon them. When used, they blur the point and slip and slither all over the place so that they focus as much on the false as on the true.

Man is so fashioned that he has no reliable guide of truth, but instead has many to guide him falsely. But the most intriguing source of his errors is the struggle between the senses and reason. (44-82)

22. Man is nothing but a subject so naturally full of error that it can only be eradicated through grace. There is nothing to show him the truth, for everything deceives him. The two so-called principles of truth—reason and the senses—are not only not genuine but are engaged in mutual deception. Through false appearances the senses deceive reason. And just as they trick the soul, they are in turn tricked by it. It takes its revenge. The senses are influenced by the passions, which produce false impressions. (45-83)

23. Reason as a supreme mind in the world is not so independent as to be impervious to whatever distractions are going on. It takes but the first noise in his neighborhood to distract his attention. There is no need to fire a cannon, for the mere creaking of a weather vane or a pulley is enough.

Do not be surprised if his reasoning is not too sound at that moment, for even if a fly buzzes in his ear it will be enough to

upset his sound judgment. If you want him to be able to find
the truth, then get rid of the distraction that is occupying his
thoughts and disturbing that mighty intelligence that rules
over cities and kingdoms. What an absurd god reason is!
How ridiculous he is as a hero! (48-85)

24. What astonishes me most is to find no one surprised at
his or her own weakness. For people act similarly in
following their professions, without giving thought to
whether it is good, but confident that it is all right.
Continually disappointed, they are led on by an absurd sense
of humility to believe they are to blame, instead of seeing that
it comes from the very discipline they are pursuing. It is a
good thing for the reputation of cynicism that there are so
many people of this kind who are not skeptical, to show that
man is capable of having such excessive opinions of human
decency that he remains blind to the innate and inevitable
weakness of his condition. So he trusts and follows the
course of natural wisdom. Thus nothing more strengthens
skepticism than the presence of nonskeptics. But if all were
cynics, then cynicism would be seen to be false. (33-374)

25. People are so inevitably crazy, that not to be crazy would
be to give a mad twist to craziness. (412-414)

26. Our desire for the esteem of those around us is such that
pride will dominate us even in the midst of all our miseries
and errors. We would even die gladly, provided people talked
about it. Think of all the vanity we exercise in gambling,
hunting, social visits, and all the false perpetuation of one's
own name. (628-153)

27. Vanity is so deeply rooted in a man's heart, that a soldier,
a criminal, a cook, or a porter will boast and expect to have
admirers. Even philosophers want them. Those who write

against such will themselves want to enjoy the prestige of having so written, so that they too are seeking from their audience and really saying, "I want the same thing, but this time from my readers." (627-150)

28. Yet animals do not admire each other as people do. A horse does not admire its companion. It's not that they do not compete against each other in a race, but this doesn't matter, for back in the stable the clumsier and less fleet of foot does not for that reason give away his oats to the other, as men want others to do for them. The exercise of their agility has its own reward. (685-401)

29. But mankind is not satisfied with the life we have in ourselves, within our own being. Instead, we want to lead an imaginary life in the eyes of others, and so we are constantly trying to make impressions. We strive to embellish and improve our image, and so neglect the true self. So if we are at peace, or generous, or loyal, we are anxious to let it be known so that we can attach these virtues to our imaginary existence. Indeed, we prefer to detach them from our real self so as to project them upon the other. Cheerfully we would be cowards if that was the way we could acquire a reputation for bravery! How obvious is the evidence of our own emptiness that we are not satisfied with one without the other, and often exchange our true self for the false self! For anyone who would not die to save his honor would be looked upon as a scoundrel. (806-147)

30. Fame is so sweet that we love anything associated with it, even death itself. (37-158)

31. Even if we lift the heel of our shoe, we exclaim, "How well made it is! What a skillful cobbler!" And so we go on indicating where our inclinations come from, and even the

choice we make of careers. "What a lot that man drinks! How little that man drinks!" It's in this way that people are made either temperate or drunkards, soldiers or cowards. (35-117)

32. The most important thing in our lives is the choice of our profession, yet it is chance that decides it so often. For it is custom that makes masons, or soldiers, or roofers. "He is an excellent roofer," they say. Speaking of soldiers, "They are quite mad," while others will contradict this and say: "Nothing is so great as war, and in comparison everything else is worthless." So it is in hearing people praise our professions from our childhood, and running down all the others, that we then make our choices. Naturally we love virtue and hate folly, so the very words will decide what we think of as right or wrong in applying them to us. So great is the power of habit that, where we were created naturally only to be men, we instead will create every kind of condition or status. So some areas are full of masons, while others are full of soldiers. Men's customs create this variety and coerce nature out of its uniformity. But sometimes nature resists and gives men their instincts in spite of all customs, whether good or bad. (634-97)

33. Man's condition is that of inconstancy, boredom, and anxiety. (24-127)

34. It is not man's nature to have a predetermined direction. Rather it has its ups and downs. So fever will make us both shiver and sweat. A chill is as much evidence of the height of a fever as the high temperature itself. Likewise with human inventions from one generation to another, and indeed with all the good and evil generally in the world. As Horace says, "change usually pleases princes" (*Odes*, 3. 29). (27-354)

35. Kings and princes are not always sitting on their thrones; sometimes they play and get bored with that too. Greatness needs to be laid aside in order to be appreciated. For continuity in anything becomes tedious. So it is pleasant to be cold so that one can also enjoy being warm. Nature acts progressively, moving to and fro, coming and going. Life oscillates. The tides of the sea go in waves, while the sun moves in its ellipse. (771-355)

36. Anyone who does not see the vanity of the world is vain himself. Who then does not see it except youth, whose lives are all noise, diversions, and dreams about the future? Take away their diversion and you will find them bored to extremity. Then they sense their emptiness without recognizing it rationally. For nothing can be more miserable than to be intolerably depressed as soon as one is reduced to introspection with no means of distraction. (36-164)

37. Men spend their time chasing a ball or a hare. Such is the very sport of kings. (39-141)

38. A trifling thing will console us because a trifling thing upsets us. (43-136)

39. We never live only in the present. We remember the past and we look forward to the future. If we find it too slow in coming we try to speed it up; or we recall the past to slow it down if it runs too fast. We are so unwise that we wander through ages which are not our own and never give a thought to the one thing that belongs to us. We are so frivolous that we think of those that are nothing and thoughtlessly overlook the one thing that exists. It is because the present moment is usually a painful one. We repress it because it hurts us. And if we find it pleasurable, we are sorry to see it pass away. We try to prop it up by thinking of the future, and think how we

are going to plan things in a context where we have no control, for it is a time that we are never sure of reaching.

So let us examine our thoughts and we will find that we tend to be occupied entirely with the past or the future. We scarcely ever think of the present, and when we do so, it is only to see what light it may cast on our plans for the future. But the present moment is never our objective. The past and the present are our means, while the future alone is our goal. With this way of thinking we can never actually live, but instead live in hope. Since we are always planning how we are going to be happy, it is inevitable that we never are. (47-172)

III
MAN'S UNHAPPY CONDITION

40. What causes us to be fickle is the realization that our present pleasures are false, while failing to realize that absent pleasures are also vain. (73-110)

41. We're such miserable creatures that we can only enjoy sensationally to see things go wrong. This can and does happen to thousands of things. Anyone who has found the secret of true rejoicing when things go well, and is not upset when they go badly, will understand the point. Instead, man's life is a constant blur of motion. (56-181)

42. Yet if our condition was one of true happiness, we would not need to distract ourselves from thinking about it. (70-165)

43. Adulation spoils everything from our earliest youth. "Well spoken! Well done! How good he is!" The children of our community who are not egged on by envy and glory become indifferent. (63-151)

44. So one must really know oneself; even if that does not help us in finding the truth, at least it helps us to run our own life. Nothing is more important than that. (72-66)

45. Job and Solomon tell us that society finds no other way of satisfying its covetousness without doing wrong to others. (74-454)

46. It is false to assume that we are worthy to be loved by others. It is unreasonable that we should want this. For if we were born reasonable and impartial, with a knowledge of ourselves and of others, we would not have this bias toward ourselves in our own wills. But we are born with it, and so we are born perverted. Everything tends toward itself, and this is contrary to order. (421a-477)

47. Every man is for himself, and with his death everything is dead for him. That is why each of us tends to think he is everything to everyone. We must not judge nature simply from our own perspective but by its own standards. (668-457)

48. The characteristic of human nature is to love oneself and to consider only one's self. But what else can it do? It cannot help its own love being inconsistent and miserable. It wants to be great and sees that it is only small. It wants to be happy and finds it is wretched. It wants to be perfect and sees itself full of imperfections. It wants to be the object of other people's love and esteem and sees that its faults deserve only their dislike and contempt. Finding itself in this predicament, it reacts in the most unjust and criminal passion imaginable. For it conceives a deadly hatred for the truth that would rebuke it and convince it of its faults. It would like to eliminate this truth, and not being able to destroy it, it represses it as much as it can in the consciousness of itself and of others. So it takes every precaution to hide its own faults from itself and from others, and cannot bear to have them pointed out or even noticed.

Unquestionably it is an evil to be so full of faults, but it is a still greater evil to be full of them and yet unwilling to acknowledge them, since this results in the further evil of deliberate self-delusion. We do not want others to deceive us.

But at the same time we do not think it is right for them to think well of themselves more than they deserve. It is therefore not right either that we should deceive them or want them to esteem us more than we deserve.

So when they merely show that they have faults and bad habits which we share, it is obvious they do us no wrong, since they are not responsible for them. Actually they do us good by helping to expose them and so enable us to escape from them if we would but see. So we ought not to be annoyed that they know and despise us because of our faults, because it is right that they should know us for who we really are and despise us if indeed we are despicable.

Such feelings arise from a heart full of righteousness and justice. So what should we say of ourselves, seeing it is quite differently disposed? For is it not so that we tend to hate truth and those who tell it to us, and we like rather to be deceived to our own advantage, and want to be esteemed by them other than we actually are? Here is evidence of this tendency which appalls me. The Roman Catholic church does not oblige us to reveal our sins indiscriminately to everyone. It permits us to remain hidden from all others with one exception, to whom it bids us reveal our innermost heart and show ourselves for who we really are. This is the only man in the world it orders us to disillusion. It puts on him the responsibility to keep inviolable secrecy, which means he might as well not possess the knowledge of us that he really has. Can anything milder and softer be imagined? Yet such is man's corruption that he finds even this law to be harsh. And this is one of the major reasons why such a large part of Europe has revolted against the church.

How unreasonable and unrighteous is the heart of man that he should resent even the obligation to behave to one person in a righteous way; and indeed not to do this to everyone! For can we really believe it is right to deceive others?

This aversion for the truth occurs at differing levels, but it exists in all of us to some degree because it is inseparable from self-love. It is this false sensitivity which makes those who have to correct others choose such devious ways and qualifications in order to avoid giving offense. They have to minimize our faults, pretend to excuse them, and to mix this with praise and marks of affection and esteem. Even then, such a medicine still tastes bitter to self-love, which will take as little of it as possible, and always with disgust. Often it will also have secret resentment against those who administered it.

The result is that anyone who desires to win our affection will avoid rendering us this service which he knows to be unwelcome. We tend to be treated as we want to be treated. For we hate the truth and it is kept from us. Instead, we desire to be flattered and so we are flattered; we like to be deceived and we are deceived.

That is why the more promotion we seek to have on fortune's ladder takes us further away from the truth, because people become increasingly more wary of offending those whose friendship is deemed most useful and see enmity as most dangerous. So a prince could be the laughingstock and yet the only one who doesn't know it. This is not surprising. For telling the truth is useful to the hearer but harmful to those who tell it, because they will incur such odium. So those who live with princes prefer their own interests to that of the prince they serve. They have no desire to benefit him by harming themselves.

The tragedy of this is no doubt greater and more common among those who are more successful in life, but humble folk are not exempt either, because we all have some interest in being accepted. So human life is nothing but a perpetual illusion. There is nothing but mutual deception and flattery. No one talks about us in our presence as he would in our absence. Human relations are only based upon this mutual deception. Few friendships could survive if everyone knew what his friend said about him behind his back, even though he spoke sincerely and objectively.

Therefore man is nothing but disguise, falsity, and hypocrisy, both in regard to others as well as to himself. He does not want to be told the truth. He avoids telling it to others. All of these tendencies, so far distant from justice and reason, are naturally rooted in his own heart. (978-100)

49. "Self is despicable. You cover it up, Mitton [Daniel Mitton, a worldly gambler and friend of Pascal], but that does not mean it is taken away. You still remain despicable."

"That is not so, because by being obliging to everyone as we are, we give them no cause of offense."

"Yes, that's true enough, if the only despicable thing about the self were the unpleasantness it causes us. But if I hate it because it is wrong, then that makes it the center of everything, and I shall go on hating it.

"In a word, the self has two features: It is unjust in itself in making itself the center of everything, and it is a nuisance to others in that it tries to dominate them, for each self is the enemy of all others and would like to tyrannize them. You take away the nuisance but not the injustice.

"So, you do not make it attractive to those who hate it for being unjust. You only make it pleasing to unjust people who no longer see it as their enemy. So you remain unjust, and you can only please unjust people." (597-455)

50. Mitton knows quite well that human nature is corrupted and that men are opposed to integrity. But he doesn't understand why men cannot transcend this. (642-448)

51. Even the poorest child will say, "This is my dog, this is my place in the sun." This is the origin and symbol of how man would usurp everything. (64-295)

52. So tyranny consists in the desire to dominate everything regardless of order. In the various attributes of mankind, such as strength, beauty, sensibility, and piety, each is master of his own house but nowhere else. Sometimes they conflict and the strong or the handsome will strive to dominate, but this is absurd because their mastery is of different kinds. So they do not understand each other and their mistake lies in wanting to rule everything. Nothing can do this, not even strength.

Brute power has no effect upon the world of scholarship and only governs external actions. So these human tendencies are false.

Tyranny means wanting to have by one means what can only be had by another. We have to pay different custom tolls for different kinds of merit. We must love charm, or fear strength, or believe in knowledge. These dues must be paid. It is wrong to refuse them and wrong to demand any others. So we see how false and tyrannical are some of these arguments: "I am beautiful, so you must fear me. I am strong, so you must love me." Likewise, it is false and tyrannical to say: "He is not strong, so I won't respect him. He is not clever, so I will not fear him." (58-332)

53. Laws are often unreasonable, so there is a tendency to want to break away from them; but in the process the law breaker may become all the more deceived.

For what basis will he take for the economy of the world he wants to rule? Will it be the whim of everyone? What confusion there would be! Will it be justice? Yet he does not know what that means. For if he did, he would certainly never have laid down this most commonly accepted of all human maxims: Each one should follow the customs of his own country. True justice would enthrall all the peoples of the world with its splendor. Lawgivers would not take their model from the whims and fancies either of Persians or of Germans as a substitute for consistent justice. We should see this established in every country of the world, in every period of history, whereas in fact we see that what is considered right or wrong changes color as it changes climate. Three degrees of latitude upset the whole framework of jurisprudence and the shift of one meridian determines what is true. Basic laws change when they have been in the statute book only for a few years, so that even law has its fashions. It's an extraordinary kind of justice whose limits are marked by a river boundary where it is true on this side and false on the other.

It is acknowledged that justice does not lie within these customs, but resides in natural laws common to every nation.

If there was just one law that was universal, then people would maintain this obstinately; but the absurdity is that man's whims have such infinite variety that there is not a single universal one.

Thus larceny, incest, infanticide, parricide, have all at some time or other been reckoned virtuous. So can there be anything more absurd than that a man has the right to kill me because he lives on the other side of the ocean, and that his prince has picked a quarrel with me, although I have no relationship with him?

Doubtless there are natural laws, but once this fine reason of ours is corrupted, it corrupts everything. All seems to be relativized by convention (as Cicero has pointed out in *De Fin*, 5.21). It is by virtue of decrees of the Senate and votes of the people that crimes are committed (as Seneca has shown, *Ep.* 95). Just as we once used to suffer for our vices, now we suffer for our laws (as Tacitus has observed, *Ann.*, 3.25).

The consequence of this confusion is that one will say the essence of justice is the authority of the law-giver, while another will argue that it is the expediency of the sovereign, or yet another that it is present custom that is most reliable. If everything is so rationalized, nothing has intrinsic value that will not change with time. Custom is the whole of equity merely because it is acceptable. This is the mystical basis of its authority. So anyone who reverts back to its fundamental principle only destroys it. Nothing is so defective as those laws which seek to correct defects. Anyone obeying them because they are righteous is obeying an imaginary justice, not the essence of the law which is completely self-contained. It is law and nothing else. Whoever wants to examine the reason for this will find it so trivial and weak, that unless he is familiar with the intricacies of human imagination, he will be amazed that in the course of a century it has acquired so much importance and reverence.

It is the art of subversion and revolution to upset established customs by going back to their origins in order to show how they lack legitimacy and authority. There must be, they argue, a return to the basic and original laws of the state which unjust custom has removed. There is no surer way therefore to lose everything than by doing this. Nothing can be just that is weighed on these scales. Yet people are only too ready to listen to such arguments, throwing off the yoke as soon as they recognize it, and taking the opportunity to ruin themselves and those whose curiosity incites them to look at these traditional customs. This explains why the most wise among legislators used to say that men are often deceived by their own ideals. Another wise politician (Scaevola quoted by Augustine in *The City of God*) says: "Man asks for the truth which will set him free; and it is believed that it is expedient for him to be deceived!" (Book 4.27).

The perversion of truth must be camouflaged because it originally came about irrationally, and yet has now been made to appear rational. We must be persuaded that it remains authentic and eternal, but its origins must be hidden from us if we do not want to see it terminated. (60-294)

54. It is dangerous to tell people that laws are unjust, because they only obey them on the assumption that they are just. That is why they must be told that laws are to be obeyed because they are laws, just as superiors have to be obeyed because they are our bosses. That is how sedition can be forestalled. For if people are made to understand that, then they see this to be the proper definition of justice. (66-326)

55. When I reflect upon the brief span of my life compared with eternity before and after it—"as the remembrance of a guest that stays only for a day" (Wisdom 5.15)—I see the small space I occupy swallowed up in the infinite immensity of spheres I know nothing about and which know nothing about me. It makes me fearful and amazes me to see myself here rather than there. For there is no reason why I should be here rather than there, now rather than then. Who put me here? By whose command and action was this time and place allocated to me? (68-205)

IV
MAN'S BOREDOM

56. Curiosity is merely a form of vanity [or as Bernard of Clairvaux pointed out, curiosity is the first degree of pride]. Usually we only want to know about things in order to be able to talk about them. Otherwise, we might venture on a sea voyage without ever talking about it, merely for the pleasure of seeing without any prospect of being able to tell people what we have seen. (77-152)

57. A definition of man is of a being of dependence, longing for independence, and having needs. (78-126)

58. How frustrated we are when we have to give up occupations or pursuits to which we are attached! A man may enjoy life at home, but he has only to see a woman who attracts him, or to escape for a few days' diversion, and you will find him unsettled and miserable at having to return to his normal way of life. This happens every day. (79-128)

59. Man finds nothing so intolerable as to be in a state of absolute rest, without exercising any passions, being unemployed, having no diversion, and living without any effort. It is then that he thinks he faces emptiness, loneliness, a sense of inadequacy, feeling dependent, helpless, and living a meaningless life. Then there wells up from the depths of his

being a sense of boredom, pessimism, depression, frustration, resentment, and despair. (622-131)

V
MAN LIVING RATIONALISTICALLY

60. Ordinary folk have a good deal of common sense. For example: (1) They choose to be amused, and they prefer the hunt over the kill. The would-be educated may scorn and laugh at them, thinking they are foolish, but for a reason they do not grasp, the people are right. (2) In judging people by their outward appearance such as birth or wealth. The people again triumph by showing how unreasonable such distinctions are. Even cannibals will laugh at a child-king. (3) In taking offense when someone hits them, or in being over-eager for fame. Someone who receives a blow without taking offense is often overwhelmed with insults and forced into penury, while ambition is most desirable because of other benefits that it gives. (4) In taking chances, such as going to sea, or crossing along a plank. (101-324)

61. Deference for others may mean putting yourself out. This may appear to be pointless, yet it is quite right, because it is the same thing as saying: "I would certainly put myself to inconvenience on your account if it were really necessary, in fact I am already doing it because you are not." Besides, deference serves to distinguish those who are superior. If deference for others really meant just remaining at my ease, then deference would be shown to everyone and no one would be distinguished. It is in being put to some

inconvenience that we make distinctions quite clear. (80-317)

62. Lust and power are the springs of all our actions. For lust leads to voluntary actions and power to involuntary. (97-334)

63. If we are not prepared to take risks we should have nothing to do with religion. For this, like everything else, appears uncertain. Think of the number of chances we constantly take as we go on sea voyages or into battle. Of this I am certain, that we will do nothing if we don't take risks. And indeed, there is more certainty in religion than there is in our assumption that we will live to see tomorrow. We have no guarantee about tomorrow. Yet we cannot say this is the element of uncertainty in religion. It may appear uncertain that it is true, but who can dare say it is certainly untrue? Yet we work for tomorrow and take the chance that we are behaving sensibly. For as the rule of probability demonstrates, we ought to take chances.

Augustine saw that we take chances at sea and in battle, but he did not see the rule of probability which proves that we ought to do so. Montaigne saw that we are often stumbled by having inadequate thought without having adequate reason instead of habitual attitudes.

All these saw the effects but did not understand the causes. They are like those who have eyes but who don't use their minds. The effects can be seen by the senses, but the causes can only be perceived by the mind. Although these effects can also be seen by the mind, the mind can be equated with that which sees causes, just as the bodily senses see effects. (577-234)

64. Why is it that a lame man does not annoy us in the way a lame mind does? Is it not because a lame man recognizes that we are walking straight, while a lame mind assumes we are all limping? Were it not for this distortion we would feel sorry for him rather than angry.

Epictetus goes much further when he asks: Why do we not get angry if someone says we have a headache, yet are very angry if someone says we are arguing foolishly or illogically?

Because we can be quite certain we have no headache and are not lame, but we cannot be quite so certain that we are making the right argument or the right choice. Since our assurance only rests on what we see with both eyes, when someone sees something contradictory to what we see, we are startled and uneasy. This is reinforced when a thousand other people make fun of our decision. For we are bound to prefer our own insight to that of others, and that is both a bold and difficult thing to do. But in the case of a lame man, our senses produce no such contradiction. (98, 99a-80, 536b)

65. [Since force tends to be the basis of justice], it is right to follow the right, but it is necessary to follow the powerful: Right without might is helpless, whereas might without right is tyrannical. Right without might is challenged because there are always unjust people around. Power without justice is to be condemned. Justice and power must therefore be combined so that we can ensure that what is right is strong, or that what is strong is just.

Right tends to be debatable, while power is recognizable and cannot be disputed. Therefore it is impossible to give power to justice, because power has tended to repudiate justice and declare it to be unjust and has instead argued that power itself is just. Thus being unable to make right into might, we have made might into right. (103-298)

66. Why is it that only the universal rules are the law of the land, those concerning day-to-day affairs and the majority decisions about other matters? It is because power is implied. That is why kings, who derive power from elsewhere, do not give way to the majority vote of their ministers. Equality of goods is doubtless just. But since might cannot be forced to obey justice, the theory has been devised that might is right. Unable to enforce justice, might is justified, so the strong tend to be associated with the just to bring about peace, which is viewed as the sovereign good. (81-299)

67. Majority rule is reckoned to be best because it is obvious for all to see, and it also has the power to make itself obeyed. Yet it reflects the opinions often of the least competent.

Ideally, if we had been able to, we should have placed power in the hands of justice. But since power does not allow us to manipulate it as we would like—because it is a palpable quality, whereas justice is a spiritual quality we can use as we wish—justice has been placed in the hands of power. So we tend to describe as just what we are forced to obey.

Hence the right of the sword is seen because the sword confers an obvious right. Otherwise we should see violence on the one side and justice on the other. (End of the twelfth *Provincial Letter*)

Thus we see the injustice of the Fronde, which sets itself up in its pretended justice against power. Likewise in the church, we find genuine justice without any violence. (85-878)

68. So we no longer have true justice. For if we had, we should not regard our submission to the customs of our country as the rule of justice. Unable to discover the just, we have instead found the strong. (86-297)

69. Justice is commonly assumed. Thus all our established laws are looked upon as just without examination once they are promulgated. (645-312)

70. So why do we follow the majority? Is it because they are right? No, it is because they are more powerful. Why do we accept customary laws and opinions? Is it because they are the most sound? No, but they are unique and leave us no basis for dispute. (711-301)

71. [To question justice therefore is to fall under the rule of force once again.] For the greatest of evils is civil war. This is bound to come where people want to reward merit, because everyone will claim to do so. It is a lesser evil if by the right of birth the succession is handed on to a fool. [One is

therefore forced to take up a third position, where one can see the strengths and weaknesses of popular opinion.] (94-313)

72. Cause and effect therefore create a constant swing from pro to con. We have shown that man is foolish on account of the importance he attaches to things that do not really matter, and all these opinions have been refuted.

We have gone on to show that all these views are sound, and as all these forms of vanity have substance, people are not as foolish as they are made out to be. This means that we have demolished the view which has demolished their world view. But now we have reached a point at which we must demolish the last proposition, and show that it remains true that people are foolish, however sound their opinions may appear to be. Not seeing the truth as it really is means finding it in places where it doesn't exist, and so their views are always unsound and misguided. (93-328)

73. One must therefore have deeper motives and judge accordingly, and yet appear to go on talking like an ordinary person. (91-336)

74. It is therefore true to say that everyone is living in a state of illusion. Although people's views are sound, they are not sound, because they imagine the truth to be found in places where it doesn't exist. There is certainly truth in their opinions, but not to the extent they imagine. For example, it is true that we should honor the aristocracy, but it is not because gentle birth is such a real advantage. (92-335)

75. Ordinary folk honor those who are of noble birth. The half-clever despise them, saying that birth is a matter of chance and not of personal merit. The really clever honor them, not because they think like the ordinary people, but for deeper motives. Pious folk with more zeal than knowledge despise them, regardless of the reason which makes smart people honor them, because they judge men in the right of piety. But true Christians honor them because they possess

another and higher form of insight. So opinions will swing back and forth, from pro to con, according to one's insight. (90-337)

VI
THE GREATNESS OF MAN'S DIGNITY

76. Yet man has greatness even in his lust or concupiscence. He has managed to produce such a remarkable system from it as to refashion it as the image of true charity. (118-402)

77. Causes and effects demonstrate the greatness of man in his achievement to produce such excellent order from his very lust. (106-403)

78. In spite of seeing all the miseries that affect us and grab us by the throat, we have an irrepressible instinct which lifts us up. (633-411)

79. Only sentient beings can be miserable; a ruined house is not. Only man is miserable. "I am the man who has seen affliction" (Lamentations 3:1). (437-399)

80. The greatness of man is so obvious that it can be deduced even from his misery. What is natural in animals is seen to be wretchedness in man. From this we can recognize that since his nature today resembles that of the animals, he has fallen from a better state which in former times was more appropriate to him. Who does not feel more unhappy at not being a king except a king who has been deposed? Did not people think that Paulus-Emilius was unhappy at no longer

being consul? On the contrary, they all thought he had been fortunate to have been consul at all, because it is not an office one has for life. Yet people thought Perseus was unfortunate when he was no longer king, because it is natural for a king to remain so the whole of his life, and it was strange that he could bear to go on living without kingship. Who considers himself unhappy because he possesses only one mouth? Yet who would not be unhappy if he had only one eye? No one, perhaps, has ever taken it into his mind to fret over not having three eyes. But man is inconsolable if he has no eyesight. (117-409)

81. All these examples of human misery prove his greatness. It is the misery of a great lord, the wretchedness of a dispossessed king. (116-398)

82. Thought constitutes man's greatness. (759-346)

83. Man is obviously made in order to think. This is the whole of his dignity and merit, and it is his whole duty to think as he ought. Now the sequence of thought is to begin with ourselves, and with our Author as well as our end. So what does the world think about? Never about such things, but instead about dancing, playing the flute, singing, writing verse, tilting at the ring, and fighting, and even becoming king, without thinking what it means either to be a king or to be a man. (620-146)

84. I can easily imagine a man who is without hands, feet, or even head. For only experience teaches us that the head is more necessary than the feet. But I cannot imagine a man who is without thought; he would be a stone or a brute animal. (111-339)

85. Man is a thinking reed. It is not from space that I seek my dignity, but from the control of my mind. I would not have more mentality by the mere possession of more land. By means of space the universe contains me, and indeed

swallows me up like a mere speck. But it is by means of thought that I can comprehend the universe. (113-348)

86. So man's greatness comes from knowing that he is wretched, for a tree does not know it is wretched. Thus it is wretched to know that one is wretched, but it is a sign of our true greatness to know that we are wretched. (114-397)

87. In thought all man's dignity consists. But what is this thought? How foolish it is! Thought is admirable and incomparable by its very nature. Yet it must have strange defects to have become the object of contempt, for it does have such faults that nothing can be more ridiculous. How great it is by its nature, yet how vile it is by its faults! (756-365)

88. The most despicable feature of man is his lust for glory, and yet it is just this that most clearly demonstrates his grandeur. For whatever possession he may own upon earth, or whatever health or essential pleasure he may enjoy, he remains dissatisfied unless he enjoys the good opinion of his colleagues. So highly does he view human reason that whatever privilege he may enjoy on earth, unless he also enjoys a privileged position in human estimation, he will never be happy. This is the finest viewpoint he can have on earth, and nothing will deter him from this desire. This is the most indelible quality in the human heart.

   Those who most despise mankind, and put man on the same level as animals, still want to be admired and trusted by their fellows. So they contradict themselves by their own feelings. For their nature—which is stronger than anything else—convinces them most effectively of man's greatness, even though their reason may convince them of human degradation. (470-404)

89. Our idea of the greatness of man's soul is so high, we cannot bear to be despised and not to enjoy the esteem of a single soul. All the happiness of men lies in such personal esteem. (411-400)

90. [We cannot afford to be completely skeptical.] It is curious that we cannot define things without also making them obscure. So we go on talking about them all the time. For we assume everybody else thinks of them in the same way as we do. But that is a big assumption, for which we have no evidence. Indeed, I observe that we apply these words in a particular context, and yet every time two people are viewing the same object and using even the same words to express what they have seen, they will view it differently. Such conformity of reasoning does suggest the universality of thought, yet lacking the absolute force of total conviction, for we know that the same conclusions may be drawn from different assumptions.

This is enough to cloud the issue, although it does not completely eliminate the natural light of reason which gives us certainty in so many matters. The Platonists would have wagered on it, but that makes the light dimmer and upsets the dogmatists, to the advantage of those skeptics who prefer to stand for an ambiguity about reality and enjoy a certain dubious obscurity from which our doubts cannot remove all light, any more than our natural light can dispel all darkness. (109-392)

91. Instinct and reason are two signs of our dual nature. (112-344)

92. With instinct and reason we have an incapacity for proving anything which no amount of dogmatism can overcome. Yet we have an idea of truth which no amount of skepticism can overcome. (406-395)

93. We come to know the truth, not only with reason, but also with the heart. It is through the latter that we know first principles, and it is in vain that reason can try to deny them. So the skeptics who try to do nothing else, labor ineffectively. We know we are not dreaming, but however unable we may be to prove it rationally, our inability doesn't do anything but expose the weakness of our reasoning faculty, and not the

uncertainty of all our knowledge. For knowledge of first principles, like space, time, motion, number, is as dependable as any derived through reason. It is then on such knowledge, which comes from the heart and instinct, that reason has to depend and base all its argument. The heart knows intuitively that there are three spatial dimensions and that numbers are infinite, and reason goes on to show that there are no two square numbers one of which is double the other. For principles are known by intuition, whereas propositions are inferred, yet all with certainty though in differing ways. And it is just as useless and ridiculous for reason to demand of the heart proofs of its first principles in order to agree with them, as it would be for the heart to demand of reason an intuitive knowledge of all its propositions before it accepts them.

Its limitations only serve to humble reason, which would like to be judge of everything, yet not to undermine our certainty, as though reason alone were capable of providing us with instruction. On the contrary, would to God that we never needed it and that we knew everything by intuition! But this gift has been refused us by nature. So much so that it has only provided us with very little knowledge of this kind. All other forms can only be acquired by reasoning.

And that is why those to whom God has given faith by means of intuition are fortunate. But to those who are without it, we can only give it by using reason while we wait for God to bestow it on them by insight, without which faith is merely human and useless for salvation. (110-282)

VII
Human Contradictions
[Man therefore is contradictory in many respects]

94. Naturally, man is credulous, yet skeptical; timid, yet bold. (124-125)

95. Man has contempt for his own life, will die for nothing, and will have hatred of even his own life. (123-157)

96. Truth is often paradoxical. We must begin with that, otherwise we cannot understand anything, and everything then is theoretical. Even at the end of each truth that we may have attained, we have to add that we are bearing in mind the opposite truth. (576-567)

97. Consider greatness and misery. Since misery can be deduced from greatness and greatness from misery, some have emphasized misery because they have taken it as evidence of greatness. But since others have emphasized misery all the more strongly because they have deduced it from greatness, all that has been said to demonstrate greatness has only served to influence some people to accept misery, for we are all the more wretched because we have fallen from a high state. Others look at it in contrast.
  Both have been operating in a closed circle. For it is certain that so far as men have insight, they find both greatness and misery in man. In brief, man knows he is

wretched. Therefore he is wretched because he is so. But he is also great because he is conscious of it. (122-416)

98. The more enlightened we are, the more we discover greatness and misery in man. With the ordinary run of men, those who are superior are the philosophers. They can surprise ordinary folk with their insight. But Christians are those who will surprise the philosophers, since only religion gives profound knowledge of something that we recognize more clearly for being more enlightened. (613-443)

99. It is dangerous to let a man recognize too clearly how much he has in common with the animals without at the same time helping him to realize his greatness. It is also unwise to let him see his greatness too clearly without realizing also his baseness. It is even more dangerous still to leave him in ignorance of them both. So it is advantageous to draw attention to them both. (121-418)

100. After showing how base and also how great man is, man is able to appreciate his true worth. Let him love himself because there is within him a nature capable of what is good. But do not let him on that account love also what is base within him. Let him despise himself because this capacity remains unfulfilled. But that is no reason for him to despise his natural capacity. Let him both hate and love himself. For he has within himself the capacity for knowing truth and being happy, but he has also within him no truth which is either abiding or satisfactory.

I should therefore like to implant within man the desire to find truth, to be ready to follow it wherever he may find it, yet without passion. But he needs to realize how far his knowledge is clouded by his emotions. I would rather that he hated lust in itself, which automatically makes his decisions for him, so that it does not blind him when he makes his choice, nor hinders him once he has chosen. (119-423)

101. If he exalts himself, I humble him. If he humbles himself, I exalt him. And will go on contradicting him until

he comes to understand that he is a monstrous being who passes all comprehension. (130-420)

102. True religion that teaches about man's greatness and misery inspires self-esteem as well as self-contempt, love and yet also hate. [Philosophers, however, tend to take sides.] (450-494)

103. Man's nature may be considered in two ways. When he is seen according to his purpose, then he is great and incomparable. Or if he is seen as the average man, then he is like a dog or a horse that is judged by the others as to how well it can run or ward off strangers. Seen in this perspective, man is abject and miserable. Each of the two ways stimulates diversity of thought and argument among philosophers because each perspective denies the other's hypothesis.

One will say: "Man was not born for this end, because everything he does denies it." The other will say: "He falls far short of his end when he acts so basely." [So while doubts cannot be resolved by natural reason, yet Christian revelation claims to have an answer.] (127-415)

104. The main arguments of the skeptics—I am leaving out the minor ones—are that we cannot be sure of these principles apart from faith and revelation, except through some natural intuition. Now this natural intuition gives us no convincing proof that they are true. We remain uncertain, apart from faith, as to whether man was created by a good God, an evil demon, or just by chance. So we remain uncertain whether these innate principles are true, false, or uncertain. For the answer must depend upon our origin.

Moreover, apart from faith, nobody knows for certain whether he is awake or asleep, for while we are asleep we are firmly convinced that we are as wide awake as we are now. We dream that we see space, shapes, and movements. We sense time passing as we measure it. In fact, we behave exactly in the same way as we do in our awakened consciousness. Half of our life, on our own admission, is spent in sleep in which we have no idea of truth, for all our feelings are mere illusions. Indeed, who knows if the other half of life, when we think we are awake, is not another form of sleep that is little different from the first from which we awake when we think we are asleep? Who can doubt that if we dreamed in the company of others and our dreams happened to agree, which is common enough, and then if we were alone when we awakened, should we not think that things had been turned upside-down?

These are the arguments on both sides. I omit to account for lesser ones, such as the skeptics' arguments against impressions left by habit, education, local customs, and so on, which can be eliminated by the slightest puff of skepticism. You have only to look at their books, if you are not sufficiently persuaded sooner or later.

I shall say something now about the dogmatists' only strong point, which is that when we speak in good faith and with sincerity, we cannot doubt natural principles. The skeptics have only one objection to this. The uncertainty of our origins, including that of our nature, means the dogmatists have been trying to deal with that ever since the world began. So there is constant conflict between men, in which we are all obliged to take sides, either with the dogmatists or with the skeptics. Anyone who imagines he can remain neutral will find that he has become the skeptic par excellence. Neutrality is a fundamental trait of their clique. Anyone who is not against them is their strong ally, and that is where their advantage appears. They are not even for themselves, for they remain neutral, indifferent, suspending judgment about everything, including themselves.

What, then, shall man do in such a state of affairs? Will he doubt everything? Will he doubt whether he is awake when someone pinches or even burns him? Will he indeed doubt whether he is doubting? Will he doubt if he exists? It is impossible to go on like this, and so I maintain that an absolute skeptic has never existed. For nature backs up helpless reason and stops it from going so wildly off center.

On the contrary, will he declare that he possesses the truth, when at the slightest pressure he fails to prove his claim and is compelled to give in? What kind of freak is man! What a novelty he is, how absurd he is, how chaotic and what a mass of contradictions, and yet what a prodigy! He is judge of all things, yet a feeble worm. He is a repository of truth, and yet sinks into such doubt and error. He is the glory and the scum of the universe!

Who will unravel such a tangle? It is certainly beyond the powers of dogmatism and skepticism to do so, indeed beyond all human philosophy. For man transcends man. Let us therefore grant to the skeptics what they have so often proclaimed, that truth lies within our grasp, and yet it is not our prey. It does not dwell on earth, but has its home in heaven. It lies in the bosom of God, and so it can only be known insofar as it pleases him to reveal it. So let us learn about our true nature from the uncreated and incarnate truth.

If we seek truth through reason, we will not avoid one of these three positions. You cannot be a skeptic or a Platonist without suppressing nature. You cannot be a dogmatist without turning your back upon reason.

But nature confounds the skeptics and the Platonists, while reason confounds the dogmatists. What then will become of you, O man, who seeks to discover your true nature through your own natural reason? You cannot avoid one of these three positions, and yet survive in any of them.

So know then, proud man, what a paradox you are to yourself. Be humble, impotent reason! Be silent, feeble nature! Learn from your master your true condition which you do not know. Indeed, listen to God! For in the last resort, if man had never been corrupted, in his innocence he would be secure in his enjoyment of both truth and happiness. If man had never been anything but corrupt, he would have no idea of either truth or blessing. But unhappy wretches that we are, and the more so if there were no element of greatness in us, we have a vision of happiness that we are unable to attain. We are aware of the reality of truth, and yet possess only the shadow. We are alike incapable of complete ignorance or of sure knowledge, and so it is obvious that we once possessed a high degree of greatness but have unhappily fallen from it. Moreover, it is an amazing thing that the mystery most remote from our understanding, the mystery of the transmission of sin, is something without which we can have no knowledge about ourselves.

For doubtless there is nothing that shocks our reason more than to say that the sin of the first man was the cause of the guilt of those who are so far from original sin that they seem incapable of sharing it. This transmission of sin seems not only impossible to us, but highly unjust. For what could be more contrary to the rules of our sorry view of justice than the eternal damnation of a child that is incapable of the will to sin, and be involved in an act in which he seems to have had so little part, as indeed it was actually committed thousands of years before he existed? Certainly nothing jolts us more sharply than this doctrine, and yet without this mystery—which is the most incomprehensible of all—we remain a mystery to ourselves. The tangled knot of our own condition was twisted and turned in that abyss. Thus it is harder for a man to conceive of himself without this mystery than it is to live without awareness of it.

This shows that God, in his desire to make the difficulties of our existence unintelligible to us, hid the knot so high up, or perhaps we should say so low down, that we are unable to reach it. Consequently, it is not through the proud action of our reason, but through its humble submission that we can really know ourselves. Such foundations solidly established on the inviolable authority of true religion enable us to understand that there are two fundamental truths of faith. One is that man in the state of his original creation, or in the state of grace, is exalted above the whole of nature, made like unto God, and sharing in his divinity. The other is that in his state of fallenness and sin, man has forfeited this first state and has become like the animals. Both these propositions are equally sound and certain.

Scripture plainly declares this when it states in a number of places: "My delights were with the sons of men" (Proverbs 8:31); "I will pour out my spirit upon all flesh" (Joel 2:28); "Ye are gods" (Psalm 82:6), while saying in other places: "All flesh is as grass" (Isaiah 40:6); "Man is like the beasts that perish" (Psalm 49:12); "I said in my heart concerning the estate of the sons of men" (Ecclesiastes 3:18).

From this it appears quite plain that it is by grace that man is made in the image of God and partakes of his likeness, while without grace he is like the beasts of the field. (131-434)

VIII
HUMAN DISTRACTIONS

105. I am aware that I might never have existed, for my self consists in my thought. My self therefore, which thinks, would never have been if my mother had been killed before I came to life. So I am not a necessary being. I am not eternal or infinite. But I see there is in nature a necessary Being, who is eternal and infinite. (135-469)

106. In spite of all these miseries man wants to be happy, and only to be happy, and cannot help wanting to be happy. But how can he go about this? It would be best if he could make himself immortal, but since he cannot do this, he has decided to stop thinking about it. (134-168)

107. Being unable to cure death, misery, and ignorance, men have decided that in order to be happy, they must repress thinking about such things. (133-169)

108. If man were truly happy it would be in unconscious self-forgetfulness that his greatest happiness would lie, like the saints and God. Yes, but is a man not happy who can find delight in amusements to divert him? No, because they come from somewhere else, and from outsiders. This means that man is dependent and always liable to be exposed to a thousand and one accidents that inevitably will cause distress. (132-170)

109. Sometimes, when I begin to think about the various activities of men, the dangers and troubles they face at court, or in wartime—which are the source of so many quarrels and violence, wild and often evil adventures as well—I have often felt that the sole cause of man's unhappiness is that he does not know how to stay quietly in his own room. For a man who is wealthy enough for all of life's needs would never trouble to leave home to go to sea, or to besiege some fortress, if he could choose to stay at home and enjoy his leisure there. Men would never spend so much on an army commission if they could afford to live in the city all their lives. They only turn to look around for people to talk with, or to compete against in gambling, because they have no enjoyment in staying at home.

But when I thought about it more deeply, when I had arrived at an explanation of all our misfortunes, and sought to discover the reason why, I came across a very cogent reason. It is that the natural misfortune of our mortality and weakness is so miserable that nothing can console us when we really think about it.

So imagine any situation you like, and then dwell on all the good things it is possible to enjoy, and surely royalty remains the finest thing in the world. Yet if you can picture such a man occupying all of these things, but he is left without any diversion so that he has to think about himself and his condition, then you will find that the tepid satisfaction he derives from it all is simply not enough to keep him going. Instead, he will be forced to brood over the circumstances which threaten his office, the revolts that may occur, and the death and sickness which are inevitable. As a result he is unhappy, deprived of his so-called diversion, and all the more unhappy than even the humblest of his subjects who can at least enjoy sports and hobbies.

The only good thing for man, therefore, is to be diverted so that he will stop thinking about his circumstances. Business will keep his mind off it. Perhaps there will be some novel and enjoyable pursuit which keeps him busy, such as gambling, hunting, or some show. In short, it will be what is called distraction.

That is why gambling and female society, war and high position, are all so popular. It is not that they really bring happiness, nor that anyone imagines that true bliss comes from the money to be won at the tables or the hare that is hunted. No one would accept such a present. What people want is not a soft and easy life, which leaves us with time on our hands to brood over our unhappy lot, or to worry about the dangers of war, or the burdens of high office. In busyness we have a narcotic to keep us from brooding and to take our mind off these things. That is why we prefer the hunt to the kill.

That is why men are so fond of noise and bustle. That is why prison can be such a dreadful punishment. That is why the pleasures of solitude are considered incomprehensible. That is why the best thing for a king is that people should spend their time trying to entertain him and provide an unending round of pleasure for him. For a king is surrounded by people whose only concern is to keep the king amused and to prevent him from brooding about himself. For though he is a king, he is unhappy the moment he begins to think about himself.

That is why men have tried to think of ways to make themselves happy. Those who philosophize about it maintain that people are unreasonable to spend all day chasing a hare they would never buy. But such have little understanding of our nature. For it's not the hare that saves us from thinking about death and the miseries that make us so distraught. Hunting does this. The advice given to Pyrrhus to try hard to meditate restfully, he found so hard to do.

Telling a man to rest is the same thing as telling him to live happily. It means advising him to enjoy a state in which he is completely happy and which he can think over at leisure without meeting something that will distress him. Those who give this kind of advice do not understand human nature.

Therefore, those who are naturally conscious of what they avoid, avoid rest like the plague. They would do anything to be kept busy. It is wrong to blame them. For they are not wrong to want excitement, if they only want it for the sake of distraction. The problem is that they want it on the understanding that once they have had the material things they are looking for, they would not fail to be truly happy. It is in this respect that we can accuse them of futility. This only goes to show that both the critics and those criticized do not really understand man's true nature.

If, however, when men are criticized for pursuing so eagerly that which can never satisfy them, their true reply ought to be that they simply want violent, headstrong action which will take their minds off themselves, and that is why they choose a charming and attractive object which will draw them enthusiastically to it. To this comment their adversaries have no answer. It does not occur to them that it is only the pursuit and not the kill they are really after. What then of vanity, the pleasure of showing off, or advancing? With the latter, we must think where you put your feet. The country gentleman will sincerely believe that hunting is a great and royal sport, but that's not the view of his huntsmen. They imagine that if they have secured a certain appointment they would enjoy resting afterwards. But they do not realize the insatiable nature of cupidity. They genuinely think they want rest when all they really want is busyness.

They have a secret instinct that drives them to seek external distraction and occupation, and this is the result of their constant sense of misery. They have another instinct, which comes from the greatness of our original nature. It tells him the only true happiness lies in rest and not in excitement. These two contradictory instincts give rise to confusion in the depths of their soul, leading them to seek for rest by the way of activity. So they always imagine that the satisfaction they miss will come to them once they have overcome certain obvious difficulties. This will then open the door to welcome rest.

This is how the whole of our life slips by. We seek repose by battling against certain obstacles, and once they are overcome we find rest is unbearable because of the boredom it generates. We have to get away from it all, and so we then go around begging for new excitement. We can't imagine a condition that is pleasant without fun and noise. We assume that every condition is agreeable in which we can enjoy some sort of distraction. But think what kind of happiness it is that consists merely in being diverted from thinking about ourselves!

We will either think of present or of threatened miseries, and even if we found ourselves adequately protected, boredom would of its own accord emerge from the depths of our hearts, where it has its natural roots, and then will fill the mind with its poison.

Thus man is so unhappy that by the very nature of his temperament he would be bored even if he had no cause for boredom. He is so vain that, though he had a thousand and one good reasons for being bored, the slightest thing, such as a game of billiards or hitting a ball, is sufficient to take his mind off them.

"But," you will say, "what is the object of it all?" Just so that tomorrow he can boast to his friends that he has played better than someone else. Other people will sit sweating in their studies to convince scholars they have solved the problem of algebra no one before them had been able to solve. Many others will expose themselves to great danger in order to be able to boast later on of some position they captured, and which in my opinion is just as stupid.

Finally, others will wear themselves out by poring over such subjects, not in order to become wiser, but merely to show what they know. These are the most foolish of all, for they are unaware of their own foolishness; we may assume the others would cease to become foolish if they realized their folly.

So-and-so gets through life without being bored because he gambles a little every day. Give him every morning the money he might win that day, but on condition that he doesn't gamble, and you will make him quite unhappy. It could be said that he only cares about the fun of gambling and not about his winnings. But make him play then for nothing; his interest will not be stimulated, he will become bored, so it is not just entertainment he wants. Indeed, a half-hearted entertainment without any excitement will bore him. He must get excited, he must delude himself into thinking he would be happy to win what he would not want as a gift if it meant giving up gambling. He must create some objective for his passions and then arouse his desire, anger, fear, for this object he has constructed, like children who are frightened of a face they themselves had blackened.

How is it that a man who may have lost his only son a few months ago, and who is overwhelmed by lawsuits and other disputes, was not worried about them this morning and no longer gives them a thought? Don't be surprised; he is completely absorbed in trying to decide which way the game will come that his hunting dogs have been so hotly pursuing for the past six hours. That's all he needs. No matter how miserable he is, if he can be persuaded to take up some diversion, he will be happy so long as it lasts. And no matter how happy a man may be, if he lacks distraction and has no absorbing passion or pastime to keep boredom away, he will soon get depressed and unhappy. Without distraction, there is no joy; with distractions there is no sadness. It is this which creates the happiness of people of high rank, because they have a number of people to distract them and have the ability to keep themselves entertained.

Make no mistake about this conclusion. For what do inspectors of taxes, chancellors, or chief justices seek, but to enjoy a position in which a great many people come to them every day from all over, and do not leave them alone for a single hour of the day to give them time to brood about themselves? When they are in disgrace and banished back to their country houses, where they have plenty of money and servants to minister to their every need, they soon become lonely and miserable, because there is no one at hand to keep them from thinking about themselves. (136-139)

110. Distraction is the only thing that consoles us for our miseries. Yet it is itself the greatest of our miseries. For above all, it is that which keeps us from thinking about ourselves

and so leads us imperceptibly to destruction. But for that we should be bored, and boredom would drive us to seek some more reliable means of escape, but distraction passes our time and brings us imperceptibly to our death. (414-171)

IX
THE PHILOSOPHERS' QUEST
FOR HAPPINESS

111. [Let us begin with the Stoics.] In seeking for the true good, the ordinary man in the street assumes that his good consists of money or other forms of wealth, or at least to enjoy distraction. But the philosophers have shown how vain all this is, and they have defined it as best as they could. (626-462)

112. (In speaking of philosophers who as Deists have God without Christ.) Such believe that God alone is worthy to be loved and admired, and they themselves have desired to be loved and admired of men. But they do not realize their own corruption. If their hearts were filled with a desire to love and worship God and find their principle delight in him, let them feel pleased with themselves. But if they find this repugnant, if their only inclination is to win men's esteem, if their idea of perfection is simply to make men think that happiness is to be found in liking them, then I declare that this form of perfection is ghastly. Why, they have come to know God, and their sole desire has been, not that men should love him, but that they should stop short at themselves! They have wanted to be the object of the happiness which men seek. (142-463)

113. What the Stoics propose is so difficult and so futile! The Stoics claim that all those who do not reach the highest

degree of wisdom are just as foolish and vicious as those who stand in two inches of water. (144-360)

114. These great mental acrobats on which the soul occasionally lights are not things on which it can dwell. It only jumps there for a moment, and does not sit forever on the throne. (829-351)

115. It's a fine thing to shout at a man who does not even know that he should make his own way to God! And it's a fine thing to say to a man who does not know himself. (141-509)

116. We are full of things that take us out of ourselves. Our instinct makes us feel we must seek our happiness outside ourselves. Our inclinations drive us out even in the absence of any stimulus calculated to excite them. So external objects are themselves a temptation to us, and seduce us even when we are not thinking about them. The philosophers are wasting their time when they say: "Go back into yourselves; there you will find the good life." For we do not believe them. And those who do believe them are the emptiest and silliest of all. (143-464)

117. Even if Epictetus had seen the way clearly, he could only tell men: "You are on the wrong track." He shows that there is another, but he does not lead us there. For the right way is to know what God wills. Christ alone leads us to it, "The Way, the Truth" (John 14:6). Three forms of lust have created three sets, and all that the philosophers have done is to follow one of these three kinds of lust. (145-461)

118. [Stoics and Epicureans, each only give half of the picture.] The Stoics say: "Go back into yourselves; for it is there that you will find peace." This is just not true. The others say:

"Go out of yourselves; look for happiness in some distraction." And that also is not true. We are a prey to sickness. Happiness is neither outside nor inside us. It is in God, both outside and inside us. (407-465)

119. This internal conflict of reason against the passions has made those who want peace of mind divide into two sets. Some want to renounce the passions and become gods, while the others want to renounce reason and become brute beasts [such as Des Barreaux, 1602-73, an infamous libertine]. But neither side has succeeded, and reason always remains to renounce the baseness and injustice of the passions. So it disturbs the peace of those who surrender to them. For the passions are always alive in those who want to renounce them. (410-413)

120. Man is neither angel nor beast, and it is unfortunately the case that anyone attempting to act as an angel ends up as a beast. (678-358)

121. All the more dangerous is their error because each follows his own truth. Their mistake is not merely in following falsity, but in failing to follow another truth. (443-863)

122. If man was not made for God, why is it that he is only happy in God? If man was made for God, why is he so opposed to God? (399-438)

123. Philosophers have not prescribed feelings proportionate to the two conditions of man. They have inspired stimuli of greatness, but this is not the condition of man. They have inspired stimuli of humiliation, and this is not the condition of man. Humility must be prompted not naturally but by penitence, not as a lasting state but as a stage toward greatness. There must be encouragements of greatness, which are prompted not by merit but by grace, and that after the stage of humiliation has been passed. (398-525)

124. No other [religion] has realized that man is the most exalted of creatures. Some, which have fully recognized how

real man's greatness is, still have pessimistic views which are natural to man because of his ingratitude and lack of courage. Others have been well aware how real is man's unworthiness, and so have treated the sense of his greatness with ridicule, which is also natural for man to do.

But some say, "Lift up your eyes to God. Look upon him whom you resemble, and who has made you so that you may worship him. You can be made like him. Wisdom will do this if you choose to follow him." "Lift up your heads, O ye free men," says Epictetus. Others say to man: "Look down, miserable worm that you are, and see the animals who are your real companions."

What will become of man? Will he be like God or will he be like the beasts of the field? What an appalling separation there is between the two! What will we then become? Who does not realize that man has wandered astray, that he has fallen from his rightful place, and that he is searching his way back anxiously, and yet he cannot find it? Who will show him the way? The greatest men have failed to do so. (430-431)

125. Man does not recognize the place he should fill. He has obviously gone astray. He has fallen from the true status, and he cannot find it again. So he searches everywhere anxiously but in vain, in the midst of greatest darkness. (400-427)

X
THE QUEST FOR THE SOVEREIGN GOOD

126. In the philosophers' debate about the sovereign good of man, Seneca says, "May you be content with yourself and the good things that are innate in you" (*Ep.*, 20.8). But there is contradiction in their advice, because they finally advise suicide. How ironic to think that happy is the life that we throw away, like getting rid of the plague! (147-361)

127. For the philosophers there are some 280 different kinds of sovereign good. (479-746)

128. It is obvious that sovereign good is something we should most earnestly seek, but when we turn to those who have the most powerful and penetrating minds, we find they don't agree. One says sovereign good consists in virtue, another in sensual pleasure, another in following nature, another in truth. "Happy is the man who can know the reasons for things" (Virgil, *Georgics*, 2.490). Another argues that it lies in complete ignorance, another in laziness, others suggest we should resist appearances, another argues that we should never feel surprised. "To be surprised at nothing is almost the only way to find happiness and keep it" (Horace, *Ep.*, 1.6.1). The skeptics in their long, drawn out study full of uncertainty come to no conclusion. Others even wiser say that it cannot be found, not even by wishing for it. So that's a fine answer!

If we ask whether this fine philosophy has come to any significant conclusions after all the philosophers' efforts, perhaps one conclusion is the soul will come to know itself. So let us hear what the prevailing masters of the world think on the subject. Have they been more fortunate in finding it? What have they discovered about the soul's origin, its duration, and its destination? Is the soul too great a subject for their feeble insights? The fact is they have not yet come to any significant conclusions. If Reason is reasonable, then she will be reasonable enough to admit she has failed to discover anything significant. But so far from despairing from being unable to do so, she is as keen as ever to go on searching, confident she has the power necessary for this final conquest. It is only by examining the effect of the powers that Reason has that we shall be able to come to a conclusion whether it really does have the grasp to be able to reach the truth. (76-73)

129. [The search is fruitless.] For we desire truth and find ourselves with nothing but uncertainty. We seek happiness and we find only misery and death. We are incapable of refraining from the desire for truth and happiness. And we are incapable of having either certainty or happiness. We have been punished by having this desire, to make us realize how far we have fallen. (401-407)

130. Yet it is good to be weary and frustrated with the fruitless search for the good, so that one can reach out one's arms instead to the Redeemer. (631-422)

131. Man without faith can neither know the reality of good or of justice. All look for happiness without exception. Although they use different means, they all strive toward this objective. That is why some go to war and some do other things. So this is the motive for every deed of man, including those who hang themselves.

Yet for many years no one without faith has ever reached the goal to which all are continually striving. All complain—princes, subjects, nobles, commoners, old, young, strong, weak, learned, ignorant, healthy, sick in all nations—all the time in all ages and under all circumstances.

Surely an examination like this which has gone on without pause or change for so long really ought to convince us that we are really quite incapable of attaining the good by our own efforts. But example teaches us little. No two are exactly the same, and that is what makes us expect that our efforts will not be disappointed this time as they were on previous occasions. While the present never satisfies us, experience deceives us and will lead us from one misfortune to another until death comes as the ultimate and eternal finale.

But what does all this restlessness and helplessness indicate, except that man was once in true happiness which has now left him? So he vainly searches, but finds nothing to help him, other than to see an infinite abyss that can only be filled by One who is Infinite and Immutable. In other words, it can only be filled by God himself.

For God alone is man's true good, and since man has rejected him it is strange that nothing has been found in all creation to take his place. The stars, the sky, the world, the elements, plants, cabbages, leeks, animals, insects, calves, serpents, fever, disease, war, famine, vice, adultery, incest. Since he lost his true good, man is capable of seeing it in any object, even to his own destruction, although it is so different from what God ordained for him.

Some seek their good in authority, some in scholarship and knowledge, some in pleasure. Others who have come closer to it have found it impossible that this universal good, desired by all men, should be attached to any one object that can be possessed by an individual. Instead it often causes their possessors more grief than enjoyment. They have realized that true good is something to be possessed by all without loss or envy, and that no one should be able to lose it against his will. They reason that this desire is natural to man, since all mankind inevitably desires it, and cannot be without it. (148-428)

PART TWO

THE HUMAN INITIATIVE OF REASONING

XI

INTRODUCTION: ON THE CONTRADICTORY NATURE OF MAN
[PROBABLY LECTURE NOTES GIVEN AT PORT-ROYAL]

132. The greatness and the misery of man are both so evident. True religion must teach us that there is in man some fundamental principle of his greatness, as well as some great deeply rooted principle of his misery. For true religion to really search our nature to the depths, it must account for such extraordinary contradictions. To assure man in contentment, it must show him that a God exists whom we are bound to love. It must demonstrate that our true happiness is to be found in him, and that our fundamental source of misery is to be cut off from him. It must also account for the great darkness which prevents us from knowing and loving him, and so show that when we fall away by lust from loving God, we are filled with unrighteousness. It must explain the reasons for our opposition to God that is contrary to our own well-being. It must show us the cure for our helplessness and the means of obtaining this cure. So let us look and examine all the religions of the world on this issue, and see whether any other except the Christian faith can satisfy these conditions.

Shall we find it in the philosophers, who offer us nothing else for our good but those forms of good that lie within us? Have they found the cure for our ills? Is the cure a man's presumption to place himself on the same level as God? Have those who would reduce us to the level of animals, or have the Moslems who offer us the pleasures of the world as our sole good, even in eternity, found a cure for our sensual appetites? What religion will teach us how to deal with and cure our pride and lust? In short, what religion will teach us our true good, our duties, the weaknesses that deflect us from them, the cause of those weaknesses, the remedies that may cure them, and the means of obtaining such treatment? All other religions have failed to do so. So let us see what the wisdom of God will do.

As wisdom says: "Do not expect, O men, either truth or comfort from men. For it is I who have made you, and I alone can tell you who you are. But you are no longer now in the state in which I created you. For I created man to be holy, innocent, and perfect. I filled him with the light of intelligence. I showed him my glory and my wonders. Man's eye then saw the majesty of God. He was not then surrounded by the darkness that now blinds him, nor was he the victim of mortality and misery that now inflict him.

"But he was not able to bear so much glory without falling into presumption. He wanted to be his own center, and to be independent of my help. So he withdrew from my kingdom; and when he assumed to be my equal, by desiring to find his happiness only in himself, I abandoned him to his own devices. Calling upon the creatures who had been placed under him to rebel against him, I turned them into his enemies. So today man has become like the beasts, and he is so far removed from me that he scarcely retains even a confused image of his Creator. Such is the extent to which his true knowledge has been extinguished or dimmed! His senses, which are independent of reason and often its masters, have snatched him away in the pursuit of pleasure.

"All creatures are now a source of temptation or affliction to him. As his tyrants, they reduce him by force or seduce him by gentleness, which is in fact a much more terrible and destructive form of slavery.

"That is the state of mankind today. He retains a faint desire for blessing, which is the legacy of his first nature. But he is plunged into the miseries of his blindness and lust, which has become his second nature."

From this principle which I am explaining to you, you can recognize the cause of so many contradictions which have bewildered mankind so deeply, and which have split his explanations into such different schools of thought. Observe now all the impulses of greatness and of glory which the experience of so many miseries cannot stifle, and see whether they are not caused by another nature.

"O mankind, it is in vain that you seek within yourself the cure for your own miseries. All your insight only leads you to the knowledge that it is not in yourself that you will discover either truth or goodness. The philosophers made these promises, but they have failed to keep them. For they do not know what your true good is, nor what is your true state. How could they provide cures for ills they did not even recognize or diagnose? For your chief maladies are pride, which cuts you off from God; sensuality, which keeps you earth-bound; and all they have done is to keep at least one of these maladies fostered. If they have given you God for your object, it is only to pander to your pride. They have made you think that you are like him and resemble God by your nature. And those who saw the vanity of such pretension have cast you down into that other abyss, by making you believe that your nature is like that of the beasts of the field, and have led you to seek your good in lust, which is the lot of the animals.

"This is not the way to cure you of your unrighteousness, which these wise men have failed to recognize. Only I can make you understand who you are. I do not demand of you blind faith."

Adam, Jesus Christ.

If you are one with God, it is only through grace and not through nature. If you have been humbled, it is by penitence and not by nature. Hence this dual capacity. You are not in the state in which you were created. Since these two conditions have once been revealed, it is impossible for you not to recognize them.

Follow your impulses. Look at yourselves and see if you do not find the living characteristics of these two natures within you. Are so many contradictions to be found in a simple subject? Incomprehensible? Everything that is incomprehensible nevertheless continues to exist. Infinite number, and infinite space equal to the finite.

"It is incredible that God should unite himself to us."

This opinion is simply derived from realizing our own base nature. But if you believe it sincerely, follow it through as far as I do, and realize that we are in fact so vile that we are incapable of discovering for ourselves whether God's mercy may not make us capable of knowing him. For I should like to know by what right this animal, which recognizes his own weakness, has the right to measure the mercy of God and keep it within limits suggested by his own fancies! He has so little knowledge of what God is, that he does not know what he is himself. Profoundly disturbed as he is by the condition of his own nature, he has the audacity to declare that God cannot make him capable of communion with him.

But I should like to ask him whether God expects anything else of him, except that he should love God and know him. Why does he think that God is unable to make himself known, and be the object of love, since man by his nature is capable of loving and knowing? There is no doubt that he knows at least his own existence, and that he has the capacity to love. Therefore, if he glimpses in the darkness in which he is plunged, and if he can find an object of love among the things of the world, why, if God reveals some glimmer of his being to him, should he not be able to know and love God in a manner that pleases God to communicate himself to us? Although this may seem to be based on an apparent humility, there is undoubtedly intolerable presumption in this kind of argument which is neither sincere nor reasonable unless it forces us to admit that since we do not know of ourselves who we are, we can only learn it from God.

"I do not intend you to believe me and submit to me without a reason. I cannot claim the right to force you into this position. Nor do I claim to explain reasons for everything. It is only in order to reconcile these contradictions that I wish to show you clearly, by convincing proofs, marks of divinity within me, which will convince you who I am, and establish my authority by miracles and proofs you cannot reject. Then you will believe the things I teach, and you will find no other reason for rejecting them, except that you cannot know of yourself whether they are true or not.

"It has been God's will to redeem men and to open the way of salvation for those who seek it. But men have shown themselves unworthy of it, so that it is right for God to refuse to some, because of their hardness of heart, what he grants to others by a mercy to which they are not entitled. If he had wished to overcome the stubbornness of the most hardened among them, God could have done so by revealing himself so plainly to them that they would not have been able to doubt his existence, as in fact he will appear in the last days in such a blaze of lightning, and with such an apocalyptic of nature, that the very dead will rise up and the blindest will see him for themselves."

But this is not the way God has chosen to appear in the humility of his coming. Because, since so many have become unworthy of his mercy, he wished to deprive them of the good that they did not desire. It was therefore not right that he should appear before them in a manner that was obviously divine and absolutely bound to convince all mankind. Neither was it right that his coming should be in such hiddenness that he could not be recognized even by those who sincerely looked for him. But he wished to make himself perfectly recognizable to such. Instead, wishing to appear openly to those who seek him with all their heart, and yet hidden from those who shun him with all their heart, God has given signs of himself, which are visible to those who seek him, and not by those who do not seek him.

"There is enough light for those who desire only to see, and darkness for those of a contrary disposition." (149-430)

133. I condemn equally those who choose to praise man, those who condemn him, and those who live for themselves.

I can only approve of those who seek God with groans. (405-421)

134. There are only three kinds of people: Those who have found God and serve him; those who are busy seeking God, but have not yet found him; and those who spend their lives without either seeking or finding him. The first are reasonable and happy; the last are foolish and unhappy; and the middle group are those who are unhappy but reasonable. (160-257)

135. So as the condition of unbelievers makes them so unhappy, begin by pitying them. They should not be reviled unless this does them good; but usually this only does them harm. (162-189)

136. Take pity on atheists who seek, for are they not sufficiently unhappy? But inveigh against those who make a boast of it. (156-190)

137. Atheists should say things that are perfectly clear. Yet it is not perfectly clear that the soul is only matter. (161-221)

138. The ungodly who claim to follow only reason need to be exceptionally rational. What then do they say? "Don't you see," they say, "that the beasts live and die just as men do, or as Turks and also Christians do? They have their ceremonies, their prophets, their doctors, their saints, their religious life, like the rest of us." Is that contrary to Scripture? Does it not say just that?

If you are careless about knowing the truth, there you can leave it in peace. But if you desire with all your heart to know it, this is not enough. Look at it in detail. This we do not for philosophical inquiry, but when everything is at stake. And yet, after a superficial inquiry of this kind, we go out and amuse ourselves.

So let us inquire of this religion, whether she does not account for this obscurity; perhaps it will teach us all about it. (150-226)

139. At least let them understand the nature of this religion they are attacking, before they start the attack. If this religion boasted that it had a clear view of God, possessing him without veils, it would be an effective objection to say there is nothing they can discover on earth which gives them such evidence for this viewpoint. But on the contrary, this religion says that men are in darkness and live far removed from God, and that he has hidden himself from them. Indeed, this is the very name he gives himself in Scripture: *Deus absconditus* [Isaiah 45:15, "the hidden God"].

In brief, true faith seeks equally to maintain two positions. First, it claims that God has appointed visible evidence in the church so that he can be plainly seen by those who genuinely seek him. Second, it claims that God conceals the evidence in such a way that he will only be seen by those who seek him with all their heart. What advantage then is it to the indifferent, who protest that the truth is nowhere evident? For in fact, one of the objections they have against the church, that there is such obscurity, is indeed one of the realities of the faith. So instead of proving it wrong, it merely confirms the faith.

If they really wanted to attack the truth effectively, they would have to convince us that they had made every effort to find it everywhere, even in what the church has to offer for their instruction, but without any success. If they talked like that, then they would indeed be attacking one of the claims of Christianity. But I hope to show here that no reasonable person can argue in this way. Indeed, I am bold to say that no one has ever done so. For we know perfectly well how people who hold these views operate. They are convinced they have gone to much trouble to obtain information when they have merely spent a few hours reading some of the books of the Bible, and have perhaps questioned some ecclesiastic with questions about truths of the faith. Then they go out and boast that they have sought in vain by reading books and in talking to men about it. In fact, I should say to them what I have often said: Such negligence of the truth is intolerable. It is not a question here of a mere trifling interest of some stranger prompting this behavior; it is a question of ourselves and of all we have.

For the immortality of the soul is of such vital importance to us and affects us so deeply that we must have lost our wits if we no longer care about it. All our actions and thoughts will follow very different paths, according to whether there is hope of eternal blessing. For that is the only possible way of acting wisely and with discernment, if it is to decide our course of action on this point. For this ought to be our ultimate concern.

Thus our primary interest and our first duty must be to seek enlightenment on this matter, of which the whole course of our destiny depends. That is why, among those who are unconvinced, I draw an important distinction between those who strive with all their might to acquire this, and those who go on living without troubling themselves or even thinking about it.

I can only feel compassion for those who are distressed sincerely by their doubts, and who regard it as their greatest misfortune. These spare no effort to escape from the situation, but instead make their search their main and most serious business. But I feel very differently toward those who live their lives without giving a thought to the final end of life, and who are unconvinced by the light that they have, but instead neglect to look elsewhere. These don't decide an opinion from mature reflection, but merely accept opinions out of credulous simplicity or those which, though obscure, do possess a solid and unshakable foundation. Their neglect in an issue that should vitally concern them—for it deals with their eternal destiny and everything they have—fills me with more irritation than pity. Indeed, it astounds and appalls me. It seems outrageous to me. I am not saying this out of pious sentiment. On the contrary, I mean that people ought to feel like this from the basic principles of human interest and self-esteem. It calls for nothing more than what is apparent to the least enlightened among us.

We do not need to be high-minded to realize that there is no true and solid satisfaction to be had in this world. For all our pleasures are mere vanity, while our misfortunes are infinite. Death dogs us every moment. In a space of only a few years we will inevitably be brought face-to-face with the reality of eternity, which for those who have neglected it will be eternal damnation with no prospect of happiness.

There is nothing more real than this, nor more terrible. We may seek to put on as brave a face as we can, but what lies in store at the end of the most successful career in the world is only this. Let people think what they like, but the only good in this life lies in the hope of another life. We are only happy in the measure to which we anticipate it, for there will be no misfortunes to those who are completely assured of eternal life. But there will be no happiness for those who have no knowledge of it.

Clearly it is a great misfortune to be in such a state of doubt. But it is at least an indispensable duty to seek and inquire when we are in such a state. It is the man who both doubts and yet does not seek who is most miserable and most wrong. If, in addition, he feels smug about what he openly professes, and even sees it as a source of complacency and smugness, which he blatantly professes, then I can find no terms to describe such a creature.

Whatever can give rise to such feelings? What reason is there for rejoicing when we cannot look forward to anything but unmitigated misery? What reason is there for vanity in being plunged into such an impenetrable darkness? How can arguments like this even occur to any reasonable person?

"I do not know who placed me in this world, nor what the world is, nor what I am myself. I am deeply ignorant about everything. I do not know what my body is, what my senses are, what my soul is, or the very organ which thinks what I am saying, which reflects upon everything as well as upon itself, and does not know itself any better than it knows anything else. I only see the terrifying spaces of the universe which imprison me, and I find myself planted in a tiny corner of this vast expanse without knowing why I have been placed here rather than there. Nor do I know why this brief span of life has been allotted to me at this point rather than another in all the eternity of time which has preceded me, and all that which will come after me. I see only infinities on all sides, enclosing me like an atom or like the shadow of a fleeting moment. All I know is that soon I shall die, but what I am most ignorant about is this very death from which there is no escape.

"Just as I do not know where I came from, so I do not know where I am going. All I know is that when I leave this world I shall fall forever into oblivion, or into the hands of an angry God, without knowing which of the two will be my lot for eternity. Such is my state of mind, full of weakness and uncertainty. The only conclusion I can draw from all this is that I must pass my days without a thought of trying to find out what is going to happen to me. Perhaps I may find some insight in my own doubts, but I do not want to be troubled. I do not even want to put out a hand to seek for it. Instead, I shall go without fear of foresight and allow myself to be carried off helplessly to my death, uncertain of my future state for all eternity."

Who in the world would want to have a friend who argues like this? Who would turn to him for comfort in adversity? Indeed, what use could he possibly be to anyone in life?

But it is a glorious thing for true faith to have such unreasonable men as their enemies. For instead of being dangerous to it, their opposition only helps to establish the truths of religion. For the Christian faith consists almost entirely in establishing these two truths: The corruption of human nature, and its redemption through Jesus Christ. I maintain, if they do not serve to demonstrate the truth of redemption by the sanctity of their lives, at least they show admirably the corruption of human nature by having such unnatural attitudes.

Nothing is of more importance to man than his state, nothing more fearful than eternity. It is unnatural that there should be people who are indifferent to the loss of their life and careless of the peril of an eternity of unhappiness. They react very differently to everything else. They are afraid of the least things that they anticipate and feel. The same person who spends nights and days in a rage, in the agony of despair over the loss of some status or imaginary affront to his reputation, is the same person who knows he will lose everything by death and shows neither concern nor emotion at the prospect. It is extraordinary to see in the same heart and at the same time this concern for the most trivial matters, and yet lack of concern for the greatest. It is an incomprehensible spell, a supernatural carelessness that points to evidence of an all-powerful force as its cause.

There must be a profoundly strange confusion in the heart of man that he should glory in a state that is incredible for anyone to have. However, my experience has shown me so many like this that it would be surprising if we did not know that the majority of them are disguising their feelings and not really what they seem. They are people who have heard it said that it is a sign of good manners to display this attitude. This is what they call shaking off the yoke, and what they are trying to imitate. But it would not be difficult to show them what a mistake they are making in trying to create a good impression by such methods. Certainly this is not the way to do it—I mean among men of the world whose judgment is sound and who know that the only way to success is to appear decent, loyal, judicious, and capable of helping others (for mankind is by nature only fond of those who can be of use to them).

What advantage do we have from hearing someone say he has shaken off the yoke, that he does not believe there's a God who watches over his actions, that he regards himself as the sole judge of his behavior, and that he thinks he is only accountable to himself? Does he imagine that by saying all this he is giving us any confidence in him about the future? Are we likely to expect comfort, advice, and help from him in the difficult situations of life? Do such people imagine that they have encouraged us by telling us that they think our soul is only a puff of wind or smoke, and still more by telling us so in arrogant, smug fashion? Is it something to be so cheerful about? Is it not rather something to be admitted mournfully, as though it were the most tragic thing in the whole world?

If they thought seriously about it, they would see that this creates the worst possible impression, for it is so contrary to common sense, so incompatible with standards of decency, so far removed in every way from the good form they seek, that they would be more likely to reform than corrupt those who might be inclined to follow their example. In fact, if you force them to account for their feelings and explain their reasons for doubting the truth of faith, they will argue so feebly that they will convince you of the opposite opinion. That is what someone aptly said to them on one occasion: "If you go on holding forth like that," he remarked, "you'll convert me to the other side instead." And he was quite right, for who would not be horrified at the very idea of sharing the feelings of such objectionable people?

Thus, those who only pretend to feel like that would be ill-advised to repress their own natural feelings simply in order to turn themselves into the most foolish people. If they are vexed within their inmost being at not seeing more clearly, they should not try to pretend to the contrary. They need not be ashamed of such an admission. The only shameful thing is to have no sense of shame. For there is no surer sign of weakness of mind than the failure to recognize the misery of man without God. Nothing betrays more sharply a bad spirit than not to want eternal promises to be true. Nothing is more cowardly than to be brazen about it before God. So let them leave their impieties to those who are so ill-bred; let them be at least decent folk if they cannot be Christians. In brief, let them acknowledge that there are only two classes of people whom we can call reasonable: Those who serve God with all their heart because they have found him, and those who seek him with all their heart because they have not found him.

Those who go through life without knowing or seeking God obviously feel they are of so little worth that it is not worth other people's trouble; and it takes all the charity of the faith they despise *not* to despise them to the point of leaving them to their own folly. True faith imposes upon us an obligation always to have regard for them, as long as they live, and as long as they are capable of receiving grace and enlightenment, and to believe that in a short time they may be filled with more faith than we are, and that we on the contrary may be stricken by the same blindness which is theirs now. So we must do for them what we would wish to be done for us in their place. We appeal to them to have regard for themselves, and to at least take a few steps in the direction of the light. Let them devote themselves to reading a few hours out of the time they spend so fruitlessly on other things. However reluctantly they may approach this task, perhaps they will hit on something, and at least they will not be losing much time. I hope that those who embark on this inquiry with real sincerity and a genuine desire to find the truth will be so rewarded. May they be convinced by the evidences of so divine a religion which I have collected here, following more or less this order. (427-194)

[The theme of this address is glossed in the following aphorisms that Pascal also wrote:]

140. Either the soul is mortal or immortal. This should make all the difference in ethics, yet philosophers have drawn up their systems of ethics independent of this question. They debate to while away the time. They talk of Plato, to turn people toward Christianity instead. (612-219)

141. The last scene of the play is bloody, however fine the rest of it. They throw earth over your head, and it is finished forever. (165-210)

142. Imagine a number of prisoners on death row, some of whom are killed each day in the sight of the others. The remaining ones see their condition is that of their fellows, and looking at each other with grief and despair, await their turn. This is a picture of the human condition. (434-199)

143. Before we discuss the evidence for the Christian faith, I find it necessary to point out how wrong are those who live unconcerned about seeking the truth when it is something of

such importance to them and affecting them so intimately. Of all their errors, doubtless it is this which most exposes their folly and blindness, and where they can most easily be confounded by the first use of common sense and their own natural instincts. It is obvious that this life is but an instant of time, while the state of death is eternal, whatever its nature may be, and thus all our actions and thoughts must follow very differently according to the state of this eternity. So it is obvious that the only possible way of acting wisely is to decide our course of action in the light of this, which indeed should be our ultimate concern.

There is nothing more obvious than this, and it follows logically, that people are behaving reasonably if they do this. Let us then judge on this basis those who live without a thought for the final end of life, merely drifting wherever their inclinations and pleasures may take them, without thought or anxiety. They do so as if they could get rid of eternity simply by not thinking about it, and merely be preoccupied with instant happiness.

But eternity does exist, and also death. These realities threaten us at every moment and make it inevitable that we should face them, with the inescapable and appalling alternative of being either eternally damned and miserable, without knowing which of these two forms of eternity shall meet us forever.

The consequences are undeniably terrible. They risk an eternity of damnation, yet they dismiss it as if it wasn't worth the trouble to think about, or that it is something incredible—even though it has a solid, though concealed, basis. As they do not know whether it is true or false, or whether the proofs are strong or weak, they dismiss the proofs lying before their eyes, refusing to look, and choose to remain in a state of ignorance. It is as if they deliberately choose to fall into this calamity waiting for the proofs after death. They do so openly and with pride. Should we who seriously think about this not be horrified at such behavior?

To relax in such ignorance is an extraordinary thing, and those who waste their lives in doing so must realize how foolish and absurd it is by having this pointed out to them, so that they are embarrassed by seeing their own folly. This is how men argue when they decide to live without knowing who they are and without seeking enlightenment. They immediately say, "I do not know." (428-195)

144. When an heir finds the deeds to his house, will he say that perhaps they are false and not worth bothering to look at? (823-217)

145. Man's sensitivity to small things, and his insensitivity to the most important things, are surely evidences of a strange disorder. (632-198)

146. To be so insensitive as to despise matters of importance, and to become insensitive to that point that is most vital to us, is absurd. (383-197)

147. The views of Copernicus do not need to be examined more closely. But what we are discussing affects our whole life, in knowing whether the soul is mortal or immortal. (164-218)

148. Supposing a prisoner in the dungeon—not knowing whether sentence had been passed on him, and with only an hour left to find out—knows there is time enough to have his sentence revoked. It would not be natural for him to spend that hour wasting his time playing a game, indifferent as to whether the sentence has been passed. So it is surely beyond all nature that man is indifferent to how things are being weighed in the hands of God. It is not only the zeal of those who seek him that proves God's existence, but also the blindness of those who do not seek him. (163-200)

149. Those who are miserable to find themselves without faith show us that God has not enlightened them. But the others show us that there is a God who is blinding them. (596-202)

150. Atheism does reveal strength of mind, but only to a certain extent. (157-225)

XII
REASON CAN BEGIN AGAIN BY RECOGNIZING WHAT IT CAN NEVER KNOW

151. Infinity. Nothingness. Our soul is tossed into the body where it finds number, time, dimensions. It reasons about them and calls them natural, or necessary, and can believe nothing else.

To add unity to infinity does not increase it in any way, any more than a foot adds to an infinite measurement. The finite is eliminated in the presence of the infinite and becomes sheer nothing. So it is with our minds before God, or our justice in the presence of divine justice. There is no greater disproportion between our justice and God's as there is between unity and infinity. God's justice must be as vast as his mercy. Now justice shown to the damned is less overwhelming and less shocking than mercy is toward the saved. We know the infinite exists without knowing its nature, just as we know it is untrue that numbers are finite. It is thus also true that there is an infinite number, though we do not know what it is. It is untrue that it is even, untrue that it is odd, because by adding a unit its nature is not changed. Yet it is a number, and every number is even or odd. It is true that this applies to all finite numbers. Thus we may be sure there is a God without knowing who he is.

We know therefore the existence of nature, of the finite, because we are finite, and like it consist of an extension in

129

space. We know the existence of the infinite and we do not know its nature, because it too has extension but unlike us has no limits. But we do not know what it is. In the same way we may be sure there is a God who exists, without knowing what he is.

Is there not a substantial truth seeing that there are so many true things which are not truth itself? We therefore know the existence and nature of the finite because we are finite, and like it consist of extension in space. We know the existence of the infinite and do not know its nature, because it possesses extension like ourselves, but not limits like we have. But we do not know either the existence or the nature of God, because he has neither extension nor limits. But by faith we know that he exists. And through glory we shall come to know his nature.

I have already shown that we can perfectly well know the existence of something without knowing its nature. So let us now speak according to our own natural perspective. If there is a God, he is infinitely beyond our comprehension, since being indivisible and without limits, he bears no relation to us. We are therefore incapable of knowing either what he is or whether he may be. Because of that, who would dare to attempt to answer the question about him? Certainly it cannot be us, who bear no relation to him.

Who then can blame Christians for not being able to give reasons for their beliefs, since they profess faith in a religion they cannot explain on rational grounds? They affirm that it is folly to try expounding it to the world. Then you complain that they do not prove it! If they could prove it, they would not be keeping their word. It is by being without proof that they show they are not lacking in sense.

"Yes, but even if it excuses those who present such an argument and it absolves them from the criticism of producing it without giving reasons, it does not excuse those who accept it."

Let us then examine the point and say: "Either God exists, or he does not." But which of the alternatives shall we choose? Reason cannot decide anything. Infinite chaos separates us. At the far end of this infinite distance a coin is being spun which will come down heads or tails. How will you bet? Reason cannot determine how you will choose, nor can reason defend your position of choice.

Do not therefore accuse those who have made their choice of falsity, simply because you knew nothing about how it was made.

"No," you may argue, "I don't blame them for their choice, but for making a choice at all. For he who calls heads and he who calls tails are both guilty of the same mistake; they are both wrong. The right thing to do is not to wager."

"Yes," you may argue, "we have to bet. For you are not a free agent. You are committed to making a choice. Which then will you make? Go on. Since you have to choose, let us see what is of least interest to you. For you may lose two things: The true and the good, and there are two things that you are putting at stake, your reason and your will, your knowledge and your happiness. By your nature, you have two things from which to escape: Error and unhappiness. Since you must make a choice, your reason is no more affronted by choosing one rather than the other. That is one point cleared up. But what about your happiness? Let us weigh the consequences involved in calling heads that God exists. Let us assess the two situations. If you win you win everything, but if you lose you lose nothing. Don't hesitate, then, but take a bet that he exists."

"That's fine. Yes, I must take a bet. But perhaps I am staking too much upon it."

"Come on now. Since you have an equal chance to win or lose, if you are only to win two lives for one, you could still bet. But if there were three to be won, you would have to gamble (since you are bound to gamble anyway), and it would be foolish when you are forced to gamble not to risk your life in order to win three lives in a game. But in fact there is an eternity of life and of happiness at stake. If that is so, and there were an infinite number of chances of which only one was for you, you would still be right to risk one to win two. But you would be making the wrong decision if, being forced to bet, you refused to stake one life against three in a game in which out of an infinite number of possibilities, one is for you, if the prize were to be an infinity of life and of happiness. For in this game you can win eternal life, eternal happiness. You have one chance of winning against a finite number of chances of losing, and what you are staking is almost nothing. Surely that settles it. Wherever there is infinity, and where there is not an infinity of chances of losing against the chance of winning, why hesitate? Surely you must stake everything then. And thus, since you are forced to play, you must be irrational if you don't risk your life for this infinite possibility of gain, which is just as likely to turn up as risking a loss of little importance.

"Surely, it is no use saying that it is doubtful whether you will win, that it is certain you are taking a risk, and that the infinite distance which lies between the *certainty* of what you stake and the *uncertainty* of what you shall win is equivalent to the finite good which we certainly stake against the uncertain infinite. But it is not like that, for every gambler risks something that is certain in the hope of winning something that is uncertain. Yet he will risk a finite certainty in order to win a finite uncertainty without being irrational. Here there is no vast distance between the certain risk and the uncertain gain. That is not true. There is indeed an infinite distance between the certainty of winning and the certainty of losing, but the proportion between the uncertainty of winning and the certainty of what is being risked relates to the chances of winning or losing. So if there are as many odds on one side as on the other, you are playing for even chances. In that case, the certainty of what you are risking is equal to the uncertainty of what you may gain. It is by no means infinitely distant from it. So our argument carries the most important weight, when we realize that the stakes are finite in a game where there are even chances of winning and losing, and yet an infinite prize is to be won.

"If this is evident and men are capable of seeing any truth, this is it."

"I do admit it and confess it, but is there no way of seeing what the reverse side of the cards show?"

"Yes, indeed there is, in the Scripture."

"Yes, but my hands are tied and my lips are sealed. I am being forced to gamble and I am not free, for they will not let me go. I have been made in such a way that I cannot help disbelieving. So what do you expect me to do?"

"That's true. But at least you can realize that if you are unable to believe, it is not because of reason, but because of your emotions. So try not to convince yourself by multiplying reasons for God's existence, but by controlling your emotions. You want to have faith, but you do not know the way. You want to be cured of unbelief, and so you ask for the remedy. Learn then from the examples of those who, like yourself, were once in bondage but who now are prepared to risk their whole life. These are those who know the way you would like to follow, and who have been cured of a sickness that you wish also to be healed from. Follow the way by which they began. They simply behaved as though they believed, by taking holy water or by having prayers said. That will incline you naturally to accept and to have peace."

"But that's what I'm afraid of!"

"But why? What have you to lose? In order to prove to you that it really works, it will control the emotions which for you are such a great stumbling block.

"Now what harm will come to you by choosing this course of action? You will be faithful, honest, humble, grateful, full of good works, a true and genuine friend. In fact, you will no longer find yourself swamped by poisonous pleasures, such as those of lust and desire for fame. But won't you have anything else? I assure you that you will gain in this life, and that with every step you take along this way, you will realize you have bet on something sure and infinite which has cost you nothing."

"Oh, how these words fill me with joy and delight!"

If this argument appeals to you and seems cogent, you should know that it comes from a man who went down upon his knees, before he wrote and afterwards prayed to this Infinite, Indivisible Being, to whom he has submitted the whole of his own being, that God may grant that you submit yourself for your own good and for his glory, and that strength might be given to such humility. (418-233)

XIII
SUBMISSION, THE CORRECT USE OF REASON

152. Submission and the use of reason are what make true Christianity. (167-269)

153. We have to know when to doubt, when to affirm what is certain, and when to submit. Anyone who acts otherwise does not understand the force of reason. There are some who break all these three principles, either affirming that everything can be proved, because they know nothing about proofs, or doubting everything because they do not know when to submit, or always submitting because they do not know when they must use their judgment.

   Skeptic, mathematician, Christian; doubt, certainty, submission. (170-268)

154. Mankind suffers from two excesses: To exclude reason, and to live by nothing but reason. (183-253)

155. There are few real Christians, even as regards faith. There are plenty who believe, but do so out of superstition. There are many who do not believe, but because they are libertines. There are few in between. I do not include in this list those who live a truly devout life, nor all those who believe by intuition of the heart. (363-256)

156. If we submit everything to the test of reason, our faith will be left with nothing mysterious or supernatural about it. If it shocks the principles of reason, our faith will be absurd and ridiculous. (173-273)

157. Saint Augustine: "Reason would never submit unless it considered that there were occasions when it has to submit" [*Letters*, 122.5]. Therefore it is right that reason should submit when it recognizes that it ought to do so. (174-270)

158. There is nothing so consistent with reason than the rejection of reason [as an ultimate explanation]. (182-272)

159. The last step that reason must take is to recognize that there are an infinite number of things beyond it. It is merely feeble if it does not go so far as to grasp this reality. If natural things are beyond it, what can we say about the supernatural? (188-267)

160. One of the things that will confuse the damned will be the recognition that they are condemned by their own reason, by that which they claimed to condemn the Christian faith. (176-261)

161. Indeed, faith tells us what the senses cannot, but it is not contrary to their findings. It simply transcends, without contradicting them. (185-265)

162. There are two ways of persuading people of the truths of our faith: One is by the power of reason, and the other is by the charismatic authority of the speaker. We are not using the latter but the former. So we do not say: "You must believe because the Scripture says it is divine," but we say it must be believed for such and such a reason. Yet these are weak arguments, because reason can be twisted in any direction. (820-561)

163. Saint Augustine says I would never have been a Christian but for the miracles. (169-812)

164. It would have been no sin not to have believed in Jesus Christ without the miracles. "Look unto me—if I lie" (Job 6:28). (184-811)

165. When we see the blindness and misery of man, when we look upon the whole universe in all its dumbness and upon man without light, abandoned to his own devices, without knowing who put him there, what he has come to do, or what will become of him when he dies, and is so incapable of knowing anything, I am overwhelmed by fear. I am like a man carried off in his sleep and left on some terrifying desert island. There, he wakes up without knowing where he is and with no means of escape. I am amazed that people are not driven to despair over this condition. I find myself surrounded by others who are made like myself, and I ask, "Are they better informed than I am?" I am assured that they are not and that these lost and wretched creatures look around and latch on to some attractive objects to which they become addicted. But I cannot form such attachments, and considering how strongly appearances suggest that there are other things besides those I see, I have tried to find out whether God has left any traces of himself. I see a number of religious faiths in conflict with each other, yet except for one, they are all false. Each wishes to claim its own authority and to threaten unbelievers. I cannot believe them on that very basis. Anyone can do that. Anyone can call himself a prophet, but I see the Christian faith, and find its prophecies are not something anyone can do. (198-693)

166. The eternal silence of the infinite spaces [of the universe] fills me with dread. (201-206)

167. Why have limits been prescribed to my knowledge, to my height, indeed to my life, making it a hundred rather than a thousand years? What was the reason creation made it so, choosing this rather than that means out of the whole of infinity, when there was no apparent reason to choose one rather than the other, as none appears more attractive than the other? (194-208) [See No. 54]

168. *Man's Disproportion*. This is as far as our instinctive knowledge will take us. If it is false, then there is no truth in man, but if it is true, it will give much cause for humiliation, for he is obliged to abase himself in one way or another.

Since man cannot exist without believing this knowledge, before going on to a deeper inquiry concerning nature, I want him to consider it seriously and at leisure, and also look at himself, and then judge whether there is any proportion between himself and nature.

Let man then contemplate the whole of nature in her full and lofty grandeur; let him turn his gaze away from the lowly objects that surround him; instead, let him behold the dazzling light set like an eternal lamp to illumine the universe. Then let him see the earth as a mere point in comparison with the vast orbit described by the sun. Let him ponder at the fact that this vast orbit is itself but a tiny speck compared with that described by the stars in their journey through the universe.

If our vision was to stop there, however, let the imagination go beyond. It will become weary of conceiving things before nature is tired of producing them. For the whole visible world is an imperceptible atom in the ample bosom of nature. No idea can come close to realizing it. It is no good trying to inflate our notions beyond unimaginable space, and yet be conceiving mere atoms in comparison with reality. For reality is an infinite sphere whose center is everywhere and whose circumference is nowhere. In short, it is the greatest sensible indication of God's omnipotence that human imagination should lose itself in that very thought.

Let man, returning to himself, consider what he is compared with the reality of these things. Let him regard himself as lost in this remote corner of the universe. And from the tiny cell where he lodges, within the universe, let him examine at their true worth the earth, its kingdoms, human cities, and man himself. For what is man face-to-face with such infinitude?

But to offer him another prodigy, just as amazing, I would ask him to examine the smallest things he knows. Let a mite show him in its minute body incomparably more minute parts, legs with joints, veins within its legs, blood in those veins, humors in the blood, drops in the humors, vapors in the drops. Let him divide these things still further until he has exhausted his powers of imagination, and let the last thing he comes down to be the subject of our discourse. He may think he has reached the end of the microscopic in nature. Yet I will show him the infinite greatness of nature further. I will open to him a new abyss. I want to depict to him not only the visible universe, but all the inconceivable immensity of nature enclosed in this minute atom. Let him see there an infinity of universes, each with its own firmament, its planets, its earth, in the same proportions as is in the visible world and on the earth animals, and finally mites, in which he will find again the same results as in the first. Finding the same thing again and again without end or respite, he will be lost in the midst of such wonders, as astonishing in their microscopic scale as those with macroscopic amplitude.

Who can fail to marvel that our human body, which a moment ago seemed lost in the universe, itself imperceptible in the immensity of the whole, now stands out like a colossus compared with the nothingness which lies beyond our reach? Anyone who considers himself in this way will be terrified by the sight of himself. Seeing his own mass as given him by nature, supporting him between these two abysses of infinity and nothingness, he will tremble at these marvels. I think that as his curiosity changes to awe, he will rather gaze at them in silence than dare to investigate them presumptuously.

For after all, what is man in creation? Is he not a mere cipher compared with the Infinite, a whole compared to the nothing, a mean between zero and all, infinitely remote from an understanding of either extreme? Who can follow these astonishing processes? The Author of these wonders understands them; but no one else can.

Failing to perceive both these infinities, men have rashly undertaken to investigate nature as if there were some proportion between it and themselves. Strange to say, they have tried to grasp the principles of things and thence to go on to understand the whole. But their presumption is as infinite as the object they seek. For it is certain that you cannot embark on this without infinite presumption or infinite ability—indeed, as infinite as nature itself.

When we know better, we begin to understand that since nature has stamped its own image and that of her Author on all things, they almost all share its double infinity. Thus we see that all the sciences are infinite in the range of their researches. For who doubts that mathematics, for instance, has an infinity of infinities of propositions to expound? They are also infinite in the multiplicity and sophistication of their principles, for anyone can see that those which are supposed to be ultimate do not stand alone, but are interdependent, depending on others again, and thus never permit of finality. All we can do is to deal with those things that seem final to our reason, as in material things we call a point indivisible when our senses can see no further, although it is naturally capable of infinite division.

Naturally, we believe ourselves to be far more capable of reaching to the center of things than of embracing their circumference. Of these two infinities of science, greatness is far more obvious, and so only a handful of people have claimed that they know everything. "I am going to speak about everything," Democritus used to say.

But infinite smallness is far less perceptible. Philosophers have much more readily claimed to have reached it, and that is where they have all tripped up. This is the origin of such familiar titles as *Of the Principles of Things*, *Of the Principles of Philosophy* [René Descartes, 1644] and the like, which are as pretentious in fact, although less in appearance, as this more blatant one: *Of All That Can Be Known* [Pico della Mirandola, 1486].

We naturally think we are much more capable of reaching the center than of grasping the circumference, for the visible expanse of the world is visibly greater than we are. But since we are in turn greater than small things, we think we are more capable of mastering them; yet it takes no less capacity to reach nothingness than the whole. In either case, it takes an infinite capacity, and it appears to me that anyone who understood the ultimate principle of things might also succeed in knowing infinity. For one depends on the other, and one leads to the other. These extremes meet and combine by going in opposite directions, and they find each other in God and in him alone.

So let us realize our limitations. We are something and we are not everything. Such being as we have conceals from us the knowledge of first principles whose source arises from nothingness, and the smallness of our being hides infinity from our sight. Our intelligence occupies the same rank in the order of intellect as our body does within the whole range of nature. Confined as we are in every way, this middle condition between two extremities figures in all our faculties. Our senses perceive nothing extreme; too much noise deafens us, too much light dazzles; when we are too far or too close we cannot see properly. Likewise, an argument is obscured by being too long or too short. Too much truth baffles us. (I know some who cannot understand that 4 from 0 leaves 0.) First principles are too obvious for us. Too much pleasure is a bore, too much harmony in music is discordant. Too much kindness annoys us, for we want to be able to pay back the debt with something left over.

"Kindness is welcomed to the extent of the ability to repay it. After that, gratitude turns only to resentment."

We feel neither extreme heat nor extreme cold. Qualities that are excessive are hostile to us and cannot be perceived. We no longer feel them, but instead we suffer from them. So excessive youth and excessive age impair thought. Likewise, we suffer from excessive knowledge or too little learning. In a word, extremes appear as if they did not exist for us, nor we for them. They either escape us, or we escape them.

Such is our true condition, making us incapable of certain knowledge or of absolute ignorance. We float over a vast expanse, ever uncertain, always drifting, blown to and fro. Whenever we assume we have a fixed point to which we can cling and make fast, it only shifts away and leaves us behind. In following it, it eludes our grasp, slips away, and flees infinitely beyond us. Nothing stays for us. This is our natural condition, yet it is so contrary to our inclinations. We have a burning desire to find a firm footing, some ultimate, final base on which to build a tower that rises up to infinitude. But our whole foundation cracks wide open and the earth plunges into the depth of the abyss. So let us neither seek for that assurance or stability. Our reason will always be deceived by the inconsistency of appearances. Nothing can fix the finite between the two infinities which enclose and evade it.

Once this is clearly understood, I believe we shall remain at rest in the state assigned to us. The middle state, which is our lot, is always far from the extremes. So what does it matter if someone else has a slightly better understanding of things? If he has, and if he takes them a little further, is he not still infinitely remote from the ultimate goal? Is not the span of our life equally infinitesimal in eternity? What do ten years more of life do to raise such a span? In the face of these infinities, all finites are equal, and I see no cause for applying our imagination to one more than to the other. Merely to compare ourselves with the finite is painful.

If man were to think about this, he would see how incapable he is of going any further. How could a part possibly know the whole? Yet perhaps he will aspire to know at least the parts with which he has some proportion. But all the parts of the universe are so interlinked that I think it is impossible to know one without the other, or indeed without the whole.

There is, for example, a relationship between man and all that he knows. He needs space to contain him, time to exist in, motion in order to live, elements for his constitution, warmth and food for nourishment, air to breathe. He sees light; he feels bodies; in short, everything is related to him. In understanding man, therefore, one must know where he needs air to live, and to understand air one must know how it comes to be related to the life of man, and so on.

Flame cannot exist without air; so to know one, one must understand the other. Thus all things are seen as both caused or causing, dependent and supporting, mediate and immediate, all held together by a chain, linkage, that is natural yet imperceptible, linking the most distant and diverse things. So I consider it equally impossible to know the parts without knowing the whole, or to know the whole without knowing the individual parts.

The eternity of things in themselves or in God must continue to amaze our brief duration of life. The fixed and constant immobility of nature, compared to the continual changes going on in us, must have the same effect.

What causes our inability to know things in an absolute way is that they are simple in themselves, while we are composed of two opposing natures of different kinds, soul and body. For it is impossible that the part of us which reasons can be anything but spiritual, and even if it is claimed that we are simply corporeal, this would preclude even more the possibility of us knowing things, since there is nothing so inconceivable as the idea that matter knows itself. We cannot possibly know how it could know itself. So if we are wholly material, we can know nothing at all; and if we are composed of mind and matter, we cannot know perfectly things that are simple, whether spiritual or corporeal.

That is why nearly all philosophers confuse ideas of things, speaking of material things in terms of spirit, and of spiritual things in terms of matter. For they boldly assert that bodies have a tendency to fall, or that they aspire toward their center, or that they avoid destruction, or that they avoid a vacuum, or that they have inclinations, sympathies, antipathies—all of which belong to the spiritual realm. But when they speak of minds, they consider them as in a place, and attribute to them movement from one place to another, which are things pertaining only to bodies. Instead of receiving ideas of these things in their purity, we color them with our own qualities and stamp with our own composite being all the simple things we think about.

Who would not think, to see us compounding everything of mind and matter, that such a mixture is perfectly intelligible to us? Yet it is the very thing we understand least.

Man is to himself the greatest wonder in nature, for he cannot conceive what body is, still less what mind is, and least of all how a body can be united with a soul. This is his supreme difficulty, and yet it is his very being. "The way in which minds are related to bodies is beyond man's understanding, and yet this is what man is" [Augustine, *City of God*, 21.10]. (199-72)

169. Man is merely a reed, the weakest thing in nature; but he is a thinking reed. There is no need for the whole universe to take up arms to crush him; a vapor, a drop of water, is enough to kill him. But, though the universe were to crush him, man would still be nobler than his destroyer, because he knows he is dying, knows the universe has the advantage over him. But the universe knows nothing of this.

Thus all our dignity consists in thought. It is on thought that we must depend for our recovery, not on space and time, which we could never fill. Let us then strive to think aright; that is the basic principle of moral life. (200-347)

170. Cheer up! It is not from yourself that you must expect it, but on the contrary you must expect it by hoping nothing from yourself. (202-517)

PART THREE

THE DIVINE INITIATIVE

XIV

THE TRANSITION FROM HUMAN KNOWLEDGE TO KNOWING GOD

171. Jesus Christ is the only proof of the living God. We only know God through Jesus Christ. Without his mediation there is no communication with God. But through Jesus Christ we know God. All who have claimed to know God and to prove his existence without Jesus Christ have done so ineffectively. But to prove Christ we have the prophecies which are reliable and palpable proofs, and which, being fulfilled and shown to be true by events, show that these truths are certain. Therefore they prove the divinity of Jesus Christ. In him and through him, we know God. Apart from him, and without Scripture, without original sin, without the necessary Mediator who was promised and who came, it is impossible to prove absolutely that God exists, or to teach sound doctrine and sound morality. But through and in Jesus Christ we can prove God's existence, and teach both doctrine and morality. Jesus Christ therefore is the true God of men.

At the same time, however, we know our own wretchedness, for this God is none other than the One who is our redeemer from wretchedness. Thus we can know God properly only by recognizing our own iniquities. Accordingly, those who have known God without knowing their sinfulness have glorified not God but themselves.

"For after that . . . the world by wisdom knew not God, it pleased God by the foolishness of preaching to save them that believed" (1 Corinthians 1:21). (189-547)

172. Men blaspheme in ignorance. For the Christian, faith consists of two points which are equally important to know and yet equally dangerous to be ignorant about. It is merciful of God that he has given us evidence of both of these. Yet men will take the opportunity to assume that one of these points is not true from the evidence that should lead them to conclude the reality of the other. In the past, wise men who declared there was only one God were persecuted: Jews were hated, and Christians still more so. They saw by the light of reason that if there is a true religion on earth, the conduct of all morality must focus upon it. The way things are done ought to be directed toward establishing faith and making it paramount. Men ought to feel how their inmost being conforms to its teaching. In summary, the whole nature of man in particular and the whole conduct of the world in general should be the goal and focus of knowing.

But because of this they take the opportunity to ridicule the Christian faith, simply because they know so little about it. They imagine it merely consists of worshiping a God who is considered great, mighty, and eternal—which, properly speaking, is deism, a creed about as remote from the Christian faith as is atheism. Therefore they conclude that this faith is not true, because they assume in so many ways that God has not revealed himself to men as clearly as he might have. By all means, let them conclude what they like against deism; but their conclusions will not apply to Christianity, which consists essentially in the mystery of the Redeemer, who united two natures in himself, the human and the divine, in order to save men from the corruption of sin and reconcile them with God in his divine person.

The Christian faith teaches men these two truths: There is a God whom men are capable of knowing, and they have a corrupt nature which makes them unworthy of him. It is equally important for men to know both of these points. It is as equally dangerous for man to know God without knowing his own sinfulness as it is for him to know about his sinfulness without knowing the Redeemer who can cure him. Knowing only one of these aspects leads either to the arrogance of the philosophers, who have known God but not their own sinfulness, or to the despair of the atheists, who know their own wretched state without knowing their Redeemer.

Thus it is equally necessary for man to know these two issues, so it is equally merciful of God to reveal them to us. The Christian faith comprises both of these.

So let us go on to examine the state of the world, and see whether everything does not tend to establish these two major tenets of this faith. Jesus Christ is the object of all things, the center upon which all things focus. Whoever knows him knows the reason for everything. But those who go astray only do so for a lack of seeing one of these two tenets. For it is perfectly possible to know God but not our own wretched condition, or to know our own wretchedness but not God. It is not possible to know Christ without knowing both God and our wretchedness.

That is why I am not trying to prove naturally the existence of God, or indeed the Trinity, or the immortality of the soul or anything of that kind. This is not just because I do not feel competent to find natural arguments that will convince obdurate atheists, but because such knowledge, without Christ, is useless and empty. Even if someone were convinced that the proportions between numbers are nonmaterial, eternal truths, depending on a first truth in which they subsist that they call God, I would still not think he had made much progress toward his salvation.

The Christian's God does not merely consist of a God who is the Author of mathematical truths and the order of the elements. That is the notion of the heathen and the Epicureans. He isn't merely a God who extends his provident care over life and property so that men are granted a happy span of years if they worship him. That is the attitude of the Jews. But the God of Abraham, the God of Isaac, the God of Jacob, the God of the Christians, is a God of love and consolation. He is a God who fills the soul and heart of those he possesses. He is a God who makes them aware inwardly of their wretchedness while revealing his infinite mercy. He is a God who unites himself with them in the depths of their being. He is One who fills them with humility, joy, confidence, and love. Indeed, he is One who makes them incapable of having any other object except himself.

All those who seek God apart from Christ, and who go no further than the observations of nature, either find no light to satisfy them or find no way of knowing and serving God without a mediator, unless they are seduced by either atheism or deism. Both are equally abhorrent to Christian faith.

Without Christ the world would not survive, for it either would have been destroyed or be a kind of hell. If the world existed in order to teach men about God, his deity would shine forth everywhere in such a way that it could not be denied. But as it only exists through Christ, and for Christ, to teach men about their sinfulness and need of redemption, everything in this revelation blazes with proofs of these two truths.

What can be seen on earth indicates neither the total absence of God nor his manifest presence, but rather the presence of a hidden God. Everything reveals this imprint. So shall the only being who knows nature know it only in order to be wretched? Shall the only one to know it be the only one to be unhappy? He must not see nothing at all, nor must he see enough to assume that he possesses God, but rather he must see enough to know that he has lost God. For to know that someone has lost something one must see and yet not see, and such is our natural condition. Whatever course he adopts I will not leave him in peace. (449-556)

173. The metaphysical proofs for the existence of God are so remote from human reasoning and so complicated that they make a general impression on people, and even if they did help, it would only be for that moment during which they observed the demonstration. An hour later they would be afraid they had made a mistake. So "what they gained by curiosity they lost through pride" [Augustine, *Sermons*, 141].

That is a result of knowing God without Christ. In other words, of communicating without a mediator, with a God assumed to be known without a mediator. Those who have known God through a mediator know their own wretchedness. (190-543)

174. Not only is it impossible to know God without Christ, but it is useless also. They are drawn closer to him, not further away. They are not humbled, but as it is said: "The better one is, the worse one becomes, if one ascribes his excellence to one's self" [Bernard of Clairvaux, *The Song of Songs*, 84]. (191-549)

175. To know God without knowing our own wretchedness only makes for pride. Knowing our own wretchedness without knowing God makes only for despair. Knowing Jesus Christ provides the balance, because he shows us both God and our own wretchedness. (192-527)

176. The whole universe teaches man that he is either corrupt or redeemed. Everything around him shows him his greatness or his wretchedness. God's abandonment can be seen in the heathen; God's protection is evidenced in the Jews. (442-560b)

177. Everything around us shows man's wretchedness and God's mercy, as well as man's helplessness without God, and man's power with God. (468-562)

178. I marvel at the audacity with which some people presume to speak of God. In giving their evidence to unbelievers, usually their first chapter is to prove the existence of God from the works of nature. I would not be surprised about this project if they were addressing their arguments to believers, for those with living faith in their hearts can clearly see at once that everything that exists is entirely the work of God whom they worship. But for those in whom this light has been extinguished and in whom we are trying to rekindle it, the pride of faith and grace, such people see nature only by this light and find only obscurity and darkness. To such I say that they have only to look

around, and they will see in the least of things God plainly revealed. Give them no other evidence of this great and weighty manner than the course of the moon and the planets. If such an argument were to be presented to them, no wonder they would react and say that the proofs of our religion are feeble indeed, and reason and expedience tell me that nothing is more likely to bring it into contempt in their sight.

But this is not how Scripture speaks, with its better knowledge of the things of God. On the contrary, it speaks of God as a hidden God, and because nature has been corrupted, he has left men to their blindness. They can only escape from this through Jesus Christ, for without him all communication with God is severed. "Neither knows any man the Father, save the Son, and he to whomsoever the Son will reveal him" (Matthew 11:27).

This is what the Scriptures tell us when they say in so many places that those who seek God shall find him. This is not the natural light of the noonday sun. We do not argue that those who are looking for the sun at noonday or water in the sea will find it and that in the same way the evidence of God in nature is likewise. It is not. Rather it says: "Truly thou art a God that hides thyself" (Isaiah 45:15). (181-242)

179. If it is an evidence of weakness to attempt to prove God from nature, do not despise Scripture. If it is an evidence of strength to recognize these contradictions, then respect Scripture for this. (466-428)

180. It is a remarkable fact that no writer within the canon has ever used nature to prove the existence of God. They all try to help people believe in him. Neither David, nor Solomon, nor others ever said: "There is no such thing as a vacuum, therefore God exists." They must have been smarter than the smartest of their successors, all of whom have used proofs from nature. This is most significant. (463-243)

XV
THE CORRUPTION OF HUMAN NATURE

181. Without Christ man can only be sinful and wretched. With Christ man is freed from sin and wretchedness. For in him is all our virtue and happiness. Apart from him there can only be vice, wretchedness, error, darkness, death, and despair. (416-546)

182. Not only do we know God only through Jesus Christ, but we know ourselves only through Jesus Christ. We know life and death only through Jesus Christ. Apart from Jesus Christ we cannot know the meaning of our life or of our death, of God or of ourselves. Without Scripture, whose only object is to proclaim Christ, we know nothing, and we can see nothing but obscurity and confusion in the nature of God and in nature itself. (417-548)

XVI
THE FALSITY OF OTHER RELIGIONS

Christianity has a true understanding of man's need.

183. Man's true nature—his true good and true virtue—and true religion are things that cannot be known separately. (393-442)

184. For a religion to be true our nature must be known. It must recognize its greatness and smallness, and the reason for both. What other religion but the Christian faith has known this? (215-433)

185. If there is one sole source of everything, there is one sole end of everything; all from God, and all for God. True religion must then teach us to worship and to love him alone. But since we find ourselves incapable of worshiping what we do not know, and loving any object other than ourselves, the religion that instructs us in these duties must also reveal to us this inability and show us the remedy.

   Christianity teaches us that by one man all was lost, that the bond was broken between God and man, and yet through one man the bond has been restored. We are born so opposed to this love of God, which is so essential for us, that we must be born guilty or else God would be unjust. (205-489)

186. All men naturally hate each other. They pretend to utilize greed in the service of their fellow men; but this is a mere pretense, a false image of charity, for at the heart of it is only hate. (210-451)

187. Without this knowledge of God how could men be elated by their inner awareness of their past greatness, or depressed at the sight of their present weakness? Unable to see the whole truth, they could not attain to perfect virtue. Some, who regard nature as incorrupt, while others as incurable, have not been able to avoid either pride on the one hand or of sloth on the other (which are the two sources of all vice), since the only alternative they have is to give up through cowardice or escape through pride. If they realized the excellence of man, they would be ignorant of his corruption, with the result that they would certainly have avoided sloth, but then lapsed into pride. On the other hand, if they recognized that they managed to avoid pride, they would only fall headlong into despair.

It's because of this that we have the various schools of philosophy, such as those of the Stoics, Epicureans, the Dogmatists, and Skeptics.

Only the Christian faith has been able to cure these two vices, not by using one to get rid of the other according to the practice of worldly wisdom, but by driving both out according to the simplicity of the gospel. For it teaches the righteous, whom it exhorts, even to the point of sharing in divinity itself, that in this sublime state they still bear the source of all corruption which exposes their lives to error, misery, death, and sin. At the same time it cries out to the most ungodly that they are capable of receiving the grace of their Redeemer. Thus the Christian faith causes those whom it justifies to fear, and consoles those it condemns, so that fear and hope are both balanced. Through this two-fold capacity for grace and sin which is common to all, it humbles men infinitely more than reason could ever do alone. Yet it does so without causing them to despair, and exalts them infinitely more than natural pride could ever do without puffing them up. This clearly shows that the gospel alone, being exempt from error and vice, is the only faith entitled to teach and to correct mankind.

Who then can refuse to believe and worship such a heavenly revelation? For is it not clearer than day that we observe within ourselves indelible marks of excellence, and yet is it not equally true that we constantly experience the effects of our deplorable condition?

What else does this chaos and monstrous confusion demonstrate, other than the truth of these two conditions in a voice too powerful to deny? (208-435)

188. Jesus Christ is a God we can approach without pride, and before whom we can humble ourselves without despair. (212-528)

189. Other religions, such as those of the heathen, are more popular, for they consist entirely of externals; they are not for educated people. A purely intellectual religion would be more appropriate to the clever, but would be no good to help the common people. The Christian faith alone is suited to all, being a blend of external and internal. It raises the common people inwardly to the spiritual, and humbles the proud outwardly down to the material. It is not complete without both, for people must understand the spirit of the letter, while the intelligent must submit their spirit to the letter. (219-251)

190. We are indeed blind, unless we know ourselves to be full of pride, ambition, self-seeking, weakness, wretchedness, and unrighteousness. And if someone knows all this, and does not desire to be saved, what can we say about him? We can have nothing but respect for a religion that knows man's faults so well. Is it surprising that a faith which promises such longed-for remedies should be true? (595-450)

191. The corrupting influence of reason can be seen in diverse and exaggerated customs. Truth had to appear so that man would stop living within himself. (600-440)

192. The claim of Mohammed is in comparison very weak. He has no authority. So he had to invent powerful arguments since they had no strength other than in themselves. What does he say then? Simply that we must believe him! (203-595)

193. *Falsity of other religions.* They have no witnesses; these people have. But God challenges other faiths to produce such signs (Isaiah 43:9-44:8). (204-592)

194. The whole world rings out with the witness of the Psalms (See Psalm 48:4). Who bears witness to Mohammed? Himself. Jesus wants his witness to be nothing. The quality of witnesses is such that they must exist always, everywhere and wretched. For Jesus is alone. (1-596)

195. Jesus Christ was foretold, Mohammed was not. Mohammed slew, but Jesus caused his followers to be slain. Mohammed forbade reading, but the apostles commanded it. In short, the difference between them is so great that if Mohammed followed the path of success, humanly speaking, Jesus followed that of death, humanly speaking. Instead of assuming that where Mohammed succeeded, Jesus could not have done so, we must rather say that since Mohammed succeeded, Jesus had to die. (209-599)

196. I do not wish to judge Mohammed by what is obscure in him, on the grounds that it can be claimed to be mystical, but by what is clear—by his idea, for example, of paradise and such subjects. In these references he is ridiculous. And that is why it is not right to take his obscurities as mysteries, seeing that what is clear in him is absurd.

This does not apply to Scripture. I will admit there are obscurities as odd as those of Mohammed, but some things have wonderful clarity, accompanied by prophecies which have been obviously fulfilled. So the two cases cannot be compared. We must not confuse and treat as equal those things that resemble each other only in their obscurities, but not in that clarity which requires us to respect those obscurities. (218-598)

XVII
WHAT MAKES TRUE RELIGION ATTRACTIVE?

197. Jesus Christ is for all, but Moses is for one people. The Jews were blessed in Abraham: "I will bless them that bless thee, and in thee shall all the families of the earth be blessed" (Genesis 12:3). "It is a light thing that you should be my servant" (Isaiah 49:6). "A light to lighten the Gentiles" (Luke 2:32).

"He has not dealt so with any nation" (Psalm 147:20), said David, speaking of the law, but speaking of Jesus Christ we must say: "So will he sprinkle many nations" (Isaiah 52:15). Thus Jesus is for what is universal. The church offers her sacrifice only for the faithful, but Jesus offered that of the cross for all men. (221-774)

198. "Jesus Christ, the Redeemer for all." "Yes, for he offered this as a man redeeming all those who wished to come to him. If some die on their way, that is their responsibility; but for his part, he offered them redemption."

It could be argued that this is fine in this example, where the one who redeems and the one who prevents death are seen as two different people. But this is not so of Christ, who does both! "No, for Christ as Redeemer is not perhaps the Lord of all, but so far as in him lies, he is Redeemer of all." (911-781)

199. When you say that Christ did not die for all men, you are exploiting a weakness of mankind. For at once they will apply this exception to themselves, and so encourage self-despair, instead of turning them away from this to encourage hope. It is in this way that one can accustom oneself to having inward virtues by outward habits. (912-781)

XVIII
FUNDAMENTALS OF THE FAITH
AND ANSWERS TO OBJECTIONS

200. Heathen religion has no foundations today. It is said that its foundations used to lie in oracular utterances. But where now are the books that speak about this? And are they trustworthy because of the character of their authors? Have they been so carefully preserved that we can be certain they have not become corrupt? Islamic religion is based upon the Koran and Mohammed. But was this the prophet that was foretold would be the last hope of the world? What signs does he show that are not shown by anyone else who claims to be a prophet? What oracles does he himself claim to have performed? What mystery has he taught, according to his own tradition? What system of morality and what form of happiness does he profess?

The Jewish religion must be regarded differently in regard to its tradition of the Sacred Books and in popular tradition. Popular tradition's ideas of morality and happiness are ridiculous. But its Sacred Books are admirable. Likewise its foundation is admirable, for it is the oldest book in the world, and the most authentic. But Mohammed tried to preserve his book by forbidding his followers to read it. For the same reason, Moses ordered everyone to read his. And it is the same with every religion.

But our faith is so divine that another divine religion merely provides its foundation. (243-601)

201. The substance of faith consists of Jesus Christ and Adam. The substance of morality consists of self-acquisitiveness and grace. (226-523)

202. A source of contradiction. A God humbled even unto death on the cross. Two natures in Jesus Christ. Two advents. Two conditions of man's nature. A Messiah triumphant over death by his death. (241-765)

203. It is incomprehensible that God should exist, and inconceivable that he should not. Other mysteries are that the soul should be joined to the body, and that we should have no soul; that the world should be created, and that it should not; that original sin should exist, and that it should not. (809-230)

204. Everything that is incomprehensible does not, however, cease to exist. (230-430b)

205. If we argue that man is too mean to deserve communion with God, we must indeed be great to make such a judgment. (231-511)

206. Man is unworthy of God, yet he is not incapable of being made worthy. It is unworthy of God to unite himself to wretched man, yet it is not unworthy of God to lift man up out of his wretchedness. (239-510)

207. Atheists object that we "have no light." (244-228)

208. The eternal God exists forever, once he has existed. (440-559b)

209. If no evidence of God had ever existed, such an eternal loss would be ambiguous and might equally well be used to explain the absence of any deity. Yet the fact that God sometimes appears, but not always, removes all ambiguity. If God appears once, he exists forever. Thus the only possible

conclusion is that there is a God, but men are unworthy of him. (448-559)

210. It is true that man is taught his condition by everything around him. But there must be no misunderstanding, for it is not true that everything reveals God. It is also not true that everything conceals God. But it is true that God does indeed hide himself from those who tempt him. He reveals himself to those who seek him. For while men are at once unworthy and capable of God, unworthy through their corruption, yet they are capable through their original creation. (444-557)

211. What are we to conclude from all our darkness, but evidence of our own unworthiness? (445-558)

212. If there was no obscurity, man would not sense his own corrupt state. If there were no light, man could have no hope for a cure. It is therefore not only right but helpful for us that God should be partly concealed and partly revealed. For it is equally dangerous for man to know God, without realizing his own wretchedness, as to realize his wretchedness without knowing God. (446-586)

213. The conversion of the heathen was solely possible by the grace of the Messiah. For the Jews had been attacking them for so long without any success. All that Solomon and the prophets said against them was useless. Indeed wise men, such as Plato and Socrates, failed to persuade them. (447-769)

214. God is hidden. But he lets those who seek him find him. Evident signs of him have always existed throughout the ages. We have the signs of the prophecies, while other ages have had other signs. All of these evidences hang together. So if one is true, the other is also. Thus every age, having signs appropriate to its context, has also recognized the others. Thus those who saw the flood believed in the creation, and also believed in the Messiah who was to come. Those who

saw Moses believed in the flood and in the fulfillment of the prophecies. We who see the prophecies fulfilled should therefore also believe in the flood and creation. ("Additional *Pensées*," 14)

215. Confess the truth of faith in its very obscurity, even in the little light we can throw upon it, and indeed in our indifference regarding of it. (439-565)

216. Acknowledge that God wished to hide himself. If there were only one religion, God would be clearly evidenced. Likewise, if there were no martyrs except in our own faith. But God being thus hidden, any religion that does not say that God is hidden is not true, and any religion that does not explain why this is so, does not truly instruct. But ours does all this. "Verily Thou art a God that hides Thyself" (Isaiah 45:15). (242-585)

217. God desires to move the will rather than the mind. Perfect love will help the mind and harm the will. So let their pride be humbled. (234-581)

218. Contrast the blindness of Montaigne with the enlightenment of St. Augustine (*Apology for Sebond*). There is always enough light to illuminate the elect and enough obscurity to humble them. There is enough obscurity to blind the reprobate and enough light to condemn them and deprive them of any excuse. In the Old Testament the genealogy of Jesus is mixed up with so many others that appear irrelevant that it seems indistinguishable. If Moses had recorded only the ancestors of Jesus, it would have been too obvious. If he had not indicated the genealogy of Jesus, it would not have been obvious enough. But after all, anyone who examines closely can see that the genealogy of Jesus is easily distinguished through the line of Tamar, Ruth, and so on.

Those who ordained the sacrifices of the Old Testament realized how useless they were, yet those who declared they were useless did not cease to perform them. Likewise, if God had permitted only one religion, it would have been too easily recognized. But if we look closely, it is easy to discern the true religion in the midst of all this confusion.

Principle: Moses was an intelligent man. Therefore, if he was governed by his intelligence, he must have put down nothing in writing that was contrary to intelligence.

Thus we recognize that the most obvious weaknesses are really strengths. See, for example, the two genealogies of Matthew and Luke. What could be clearer than to recognize there could be no collaboration? (236-578)

219. Instead of always complaining that God has hidden himself, you should give him thanks for revealing as much as he has of himself. You will also thank him for not revealing himself to wise men who are full of pride and unworthy of knowing so holy a God.

There are two sorts of people who know God. There are those who are humble of heart and who love their lowliness, whatever degree of intelligence high or low they may have. And there are those who are intelligent enough to see the truth, however much they may be opposed to it. (394-288)

220. The world is a stage for the exercise of mercy and judgment. It is not as if mankind were created by the hands of God, but as if they were God's enemies, granted by his grace enough light to return if they wish to seek and follow him. Yet they also have enough light to receive punishment if they refuse to seek or to follow him. (461-584)

221. We understand nothing of God's works unless we accept the principle that he wished to blind some and to enlighten others. (232-566)

222. Jesus came to blind those who have clear vision and to give sight to the blind. He came to heal the sick and yet to let the healthy die. He came to call sinners to repentance and justify them, and yet to lead the righteous to their sins.

He came to fill the hungry with good things and to send the rich empty away. (235-771)

223. Jesus does not deny he comes from Nazareth, nor that he is Joseph's son. This is in order to leave the wicked in their blindness. (233-796)

224. If Jesus had only come to sanctify, the whole of the Scriptures and everything else would be oriented that way, and it would be quite easy to convince unbelievers. If Jesus had come only to minister to the blind, all his behavior would have been unclear and we should have no means of convincing unbelievers. But he came "for a sanctuary and a stone of stumbling" as Isaiah says (Isaiah 8:14). So we cannot convince unbelievers and they cannot convince us. But we do not convince them by that very fact, since we know that their whole behavior proves nothing convincing either way. (237-795)

XIX
FIGURATIVE MEANINGS OF OLD TESTAMENT LAW

Pascal's thought is delicately and subtly balanced between the use of the symbolic and the literal expressions of truth. "If we submit everything to reason our religion will be left with nothing that is mysterious or transcendent," he argues (173-273).

But, quoting from Augustine, he adds: " 'Reason would never submit unless it judged that there are occasions when it ought to submit.' It is right, then, that reason should submit when it should be submissive" (174-270). This is why figurative expressions of truth are important, as modern scholarship is recognizing once more. So Pascal asks: "Why did Christ not come in the obvious way instead of proving who he was by past predictions? Why did he have himself prophesied figuratively?" (389-794). All talk of God must in the light of his ineffable nature be the language of metaphor. "Reason's last act is the acknowledgment that there are an infinite number of things which transcend its grasp. It is a feeble affair if it does not recognize this. And if natural things are beyond it, what are we to say about supernatural realities?" (188-267).

Yet Pascal would redress the balance of thought that, unlike Greek thinking of "universals," there is also literal content in the truth of God. For God is the God of history, the God of mighty deeds on behalf of his chosen people Israel. Truth is specified, and in its literal character, it does not go against reason. As he observes somewhere, religion becomes absurd and ridiculous if we

*offend the principles of reason. So we now resume Pascal's own
language as he deals with the figurative character of the Old
Testament.*

225. We wish to argue that the Old Testament is only
figurative, and that by talking of temporal blessings, the
prophets meant other kinds of blessing.

First, this would be unworthy of God. Their sayings express
clearly the promise of temporal blessings, and so to argue that
their sayings are obscure and their meaning will not be
understood is absurd. So it appears that the hidden meaning,
which they argue was not openly revealed, explains why they
argued that there must be other sacrifices as well as another
Redeemer. They argue that it will not be understood before
the time is accomplished (see Jeremiah 33).

The second evidence is that their sayings are contradictory
and cancel one another out. If we suppose that by the words
"law" and "sacrifice" their meaning was simply "that given by
Moses," this is a glaring and gross contradiction. So they
argue they meant something else, and sometimes contradict
themselves in the same passage. (501-659)

226. There are times when we can give a good portrait only
by reconciling the conflicting elements in ourselves, and it is
not enough to display a succession of harmonious qualities
without reconciling opposites. To understand an author's
meaning, we must reconcile all the conflicting passages.

In order to understand Scripture, a meaning must be found
that harmonizes all contradictory passages. It is not enough to
have one that fits a number of passages that merely happen to
agree. There must be one that reconciles even the
contradictory passages.

Every author has a meaning to which all conflicting
passages are subordinated, or else his work is meaningless. We
cannot say the Scriptures and the prophets are meaningless.
They were certainly much too sensible. We must therefore
look for a meaning that reconciles all the contradictions.

The true meaning is not that of the Jews; but in Jesus

Christ all contradictions are reconciled. The Jews could not reconcile the end of the royal and princely line predicted by Hosea with the prophecy of Jacob (Hosea 3:4; Genesis 49:10).

If we accept the law, the sacrifices, and the kingdom as realities, we cannot reconcile all the passages that refer to these. So it follows that they must be regarded only figuratively. We should not even try to reconcile the different passages of the same author, or of the same book, or even sometimes of the same chapter, which shows only too clearly what the author intended. For example, in Ezekiel 20, it says that we shall and shall not live according to the commandments of God. (258-684)

227. When the Word of God, which is true, is false in a literal sense, it is true in a spiritual sense. "Sit Thou at my right hand" (Psalm 110:1) is literally untrue, so it is true in its spiritual application.

In such expressions God is spoken of in human terms. But that simply means that what men intend when they seat someone at their right hand, God also intends. It simply indicates God's intention, not the way he will carry it out.

Thus it is also written: "The Lord smelled a sweet savor" (Genesis 8:21), and will reward you with a rich land. This simply means he has the same intention as a man who smells your sweet savor and rewards you with a rich land. God has the same intent toward you because you have the same intention toward him, as a man has toward someone to whom he offers his sweet savor.

Again it says that "the anger of the Lord is kindled" (Isaiah 5:25) and that he is a "jealous God" and so on. Since the things of God are inexpressible, they cannot be said in any other way than what is said humanly as the church still uses them. So it says, "He has strengthened the bars" (Psalm 147:13), and so on.

So we should not attribute to Scripture meanings it does not reveal itself to have. (272-545)

The Key to Symbolism Is Given by Jesus

228. Jesus Christ opened their minds so that they might understand the Scriptures. Two great revelations were given: 1. Everything came to them in the form of symbols—"An Israelite indeed, free indeed, true bread from heaven" (John 1:47; 8:36; 6:32). 2. A God humiliated even unto the cross. Christ had to suffer to enter into his glory, "that through death he might destroy death" (Hebrews 2:14). (253-679)

229. *Symbols.* The letter kills. Everything came in the form of symbols. It was necessary that Christ should suffer and be humiliated by God. That is the cipher the apostle Paul gives to us (2 Corinthians 3:6). Circumcision of the heart, true fasting, true sacrifice, true temple (Romans 2:29). The prophet showed that it all had to be spiritual.

For it is not the meat which perishes, but the meat which does not perish (John 6:53-57). "You shall be free indeed" (John 8:36). Therefore the other freedom is only a symbol of true freedom.

"I am the true bread from heaven" (John 6:51). (268-683)

230. *Symbols.* Once the mystery has been revealed, it is impossible not to see it. Let us read the Old Testament in this light, and see if the sacrifices were true, if the line of Abraham was not the true cause for God's friendship, if the Promised Land was the true place of rest. No, therefore they were all figurative.

All these sacrifices and ceremonies were therefore either symbolic or absurdities. Now these things are clear and too sublime to be dismissed as nonsense.

See whether the vision of the prophets was confined to the events in the Old Testament, or whether they saw other things in it. (267-680)

231. The veil drawn over the Scripture for the Jews is also there for bad Christians, and for all who do not hate themselves. But how well disposed we are to know and to know Christ, when we truly hate ourselves! (475-676)

232. All Jesus did was to teach men that they loved themselves, that they were slaves, blind, sick, miserable, and sinful, and that he had come to deliver, to enlighten, to sanctify, and to heal them. This would be achieved by those who hated themselves and followed Jesus through his misery and his death upon the cross. (271-545)

233. The Jews were accustomed to great and marvelous miracles, and so having had the great wonders of the Red Sea and entrance into the land of Canaan as an epitome of the great things still to be done by their Messiah, they expected something even more wonderful, of which the miracles performed by Moses were only a prelude. (264-746)

234. The materialistic Jews did not recognize the greatness or the humility of the Messiah, whose coming had been foretold by their prophets. They failed to recognize in him the greatness which had been foretold, as when it is said the Messiah will be David's Lord, though his son (Matthew 22:45), or that he is before Abraham and that Abraham had seen him (John 8:56,58). They did not believe he was so great as to be eternal, and likewise they failed to recognize him in his humiliation and death. "The Messiah," they argued, "abides forever," but this man says he will die (John 12:34). Thus they neither believed that he was mortal nor that he was eternal. Instead, they only looked for worldly greatness in him. (256-662)

235. *Symbols*. Isaiah 51. The Red Sea, a figure of the Redemption.

"That you may know that the Son of man has power on earth to forgive sins—I say unto you, arise" (Mark 2:10-11).

Wishing to show that he could create a holy people with an invisible holiness and endow them with everlasting glory, God created visible things. As nature is an image of grace, he created among the good things in the order of nature what he was going to create in the order of grace, so that men would understand that he could create invisible things because he created visible things.

Thus God saved the people from the flood. He caused them to be born of Abraham. He delivered them from their enemies and gave them rest. God's purpose was not to save a whole people from the flood or to cause a whole people to be born of Abraham, but simply to lead them into the Promised Land.

Even grace is only figurative of glory, for it is not the ultimate end. It was prefigured by the law, and is itself a symbol of glory. But it is both the symbol and the origin or cause.

The ordinary life of man is like that of the saints. We all seek satisfaction, and only differ according to the object in which we locate it. Those that men call their enemies are those that prevent them from having it. God has therefore shown His power of bestowing invisible gifts by showing the power he has over visible ones. (275-643)

The Reason for Such Ambiguity

236. *Symbols*. The Jews had grown old in these earthly thoughts. They saw that God loved their father Abraham; that because of this God caused them to multiply and set them apart from all other people, without allowing them to intermingle. When they were languishing in Egypt, God brought them out with many wonderful signs of his favor upon them. He fed them with manna in the desert. He led them into a rich land. He gave them kings and a well-built temple in which to offer up their sacrifices of animals, and by the shedding of their blood to be purified. In the end he was finally to send them the Messiah to make them masters over the whole world, and to foretell the time of his coming.

When the world had grown old in these materialistic fallacies, Jesus Christ came at the time appointed. But he did not come with the expected blaze of glory. Therefore they did not appreciate that it was he. After his death, the apostle Paul came to teach men that all things had happened symbolically (1 Corinthians 10:11). For the kingdom of God did not belong to the flesh, but to the spirit. Men's enemies were not the Babylonians, but their own passions. God did not delight in temples made with hands, but in a pure and humble heart (Hebrews 9:24). The circumcision of the heart was necessary (Romans 2:29). Moses did not give them the bread that came down from heaven, and so on.

Since God was unwilling to reveal these things to the people who were so unworthy of them, and yet wishing to foretell them so that they would believe, he predicted the time of their fulfillment clearly. Often he did so in a figurative way, so that those who loved the symbols would linger over them, and those who liked the things symbolized would see them.

Everything that does not lead to love is symbolic. The sole object of Scripture is love. All that does not refer directly to this sole good is figurative. Since there is only one goal, everything that does not lead toward it is explicitly figurative. Thus God lends diversity to the one principle of love in order to satisfy our curiosity, which seeks diversity always leading us to the one thing necessary. For one thing alone is necessary, and we love diversity. God meets both needs by this diversity which leads to the one thing necessary.

The Jews were so fond of symbols and so fully expected them, they failed to recognize the real thing when it came at the time and in the manner foretold. For example, the rabbis took the breasts of the spouse figuratively (Song of Songs 4:5).

Christians even take the Eucharist as a symbol of the glory to which they aspire. (270-670)

237. In order to make the Messiah recognizable to good men and unrecognizable to the bad, God had foretold the manner of Messiah's coming in this way. If the way of Messiah had been clearly foretold, there would have been no obscurity, even for the wicked. If the time had been foretold obscurely, there would have been obscurity even for the good—for the goodness of their hearts would not have enabled them to understand, for example, that the closed *mem* signified six hundred years. But the time was foretold clearly, while its manner was by means of symbols.

In this way, the wicked took the promised good to be one of material wealth and went astray, even though the time had been clearly foretold. But the righteous did not go astray. Knowledge of the promised wealth depends on the heart, which calls "good" that which it loves, but knowledge of the promised time does not depend upon the heart. Thus the clear prediction of the time and the obscure prediction of riches only deceive the wicked. (255-758)

The Jewish Witness to Christ

238. *Reasons for Using Symbols.* They had to address a materialistic people and make it the repository of a spiritual covenant. To inspire faith in the Messiah, there had to be previous prophecies handed down by people above suspicion, universally known as conscientious, loyal, and with remarkable zeal.

In order to successfully accomplish this, God chose a carnal people to whom he entrusted the prophecies that foretold the Messiah as Savior and Dispenser of those worldly blessings so dear to them. And so they showed an exceptional regard for their prophets and handed on for all to see the books that foretold the Messiah, assuring all nations that he would come in the manner predicted in the books which were there for everyone to read. Thus those who were disappointed by the poor and ignominious coming of the Messiah became his bitterest enemies. The result was that of all people in the world, they are least likely to favor us, for they showed themselves to be the most scrupulous and zealous observers of the law and the prophets which they have preserved incorrupt.

Thus it is those who rejected and crucified Jesus Christ—for he was a scandal to them—who handed down the books that bear witness to him, saying he would be rejected and a cause of scandal. Their very rejection proved that it was he; his claims were proved alike by both the righteous Jews who accepted him and the unrighteous who rejected him, since both were foretold.

That is why the prophecies have a hidden, spiritual meaning, to which the Jewish people were hostile, underlying the materialistic meaning which appealed to them. If the spiritual meaning had been discovered, they would have been incapable of taking it to their hearts. Thus they would not have handed it on, for they would have lacked the zeal to preserve their books and ceremonies. If they had cherished the spiritual promises and preserved them uncorrupted until the coming of the Messiah, their testimony would have carried no weight because they would have been on his side. That is why it was a good thing that the spiritual meaning remained concealed. But on the other hand, if this meaning had been so well hidden that there was no trace of it, it would have been useless as a proof of the claims of the Messiah. What then took place?

It was concealed beneath the temporal meaning in the great majority of passages, and clearly revealed in a few—beside the fact that the time and state of the world had been so plainly foretold that they were clearer than the noonday sun. And this spiritual meaning was so clearly explained in certain passages that anyone unable to recognize it had to be suffering from some kind of blindness, imposed on the spirit by the flesh and so enslaved to misunderstanding it.

This is the way God acted. In countless places, the spiritual meaning is obscured by another meaning and revealed in very few places. Yet this is done in such a way that the passages in which it is hidden are equivocal and are capable of both interpretations, while the passages in which it is clearly revealed can only be interpreted in a spiritual way.

Hence there is no reason for falling into error, and only a carnal people could possibly have been mistaken about it. For when good things were promised in abundance, what prevents them from understanding this as true blessings but their own cupidity? But those whose only blessing lay in God relate them to God alone.

For there are two principles which battle for control of the human will: Avarice and love. It is not that avarice is incompatible with belief in God, or love with worldly goods. But avarice makes use of God and takes pleasure in the world, which love does not.

Things are described in relation to ultimate purpose. Anything that prevents us from attaining it is called an enemy. Thus creatures, though good, will be enemies of the righteous when they turn them away from God. God himself is the enemy of those whose covetousness is frustrated.

Therefore since the word *enemy* depends on ultimate purpose, the righteous took it to mean their passions, while the carnal took it to mean the Babylonians, and so these terms were only obscure for the unrighteous.

This is what Isaiah says: "Seal the law among my elect ones," and that Jesus Christ will be a stone of stumbling (Isaiah 8:6-14). But "blessed is he whosoever shall not be offended in him" (Matthew 11:6). The last verse of Hosea puts it aptly: "Who is wise and he shall understand these things? For the ways of the Lord are right and the just shall walk in them, but the transgressors shall fall therein." (502-571)

239. ". . . shall fall therein." And yet the covenant, made to blind some and enlighten others, provided a sign in just those who were blinded of the truth which should have been known to the others. For the visible blessings they received from God were so great and so divine, it was quite apparent that he was capable of bestowing on them invisible blessings and the Messiah.

Nature is a symbol of grace, and visible miracles are images of invisible ones. "That you may know, I say unto you, arise" (Mark 2:10). Isaiah says the redemption will be like the crossing of the Red Sea. God showed by the exodus from Egypt, by the crossing of the Sea, by the defeat of the kings, by the manna, by the whole line of Abraham, that he was capable of saving, of making bread come down from heaven, so that this hostile people are a symbol and representation of the very Messiah whom they do not know.

Therefore God has taught us that ultimately all these

things are only figurative, and that the true meaning relates to "truly free," "true Israelite," "true circumcision," "true bread from heaven."

Each of us finds in these promises what lies in the depths of our own heart. We either see temporal or spiritual blessings, God or creatures. But with this difference: those who seek creatures will indeed find them, but with many contradictions. We are forbidden to love them and are commanded to worship and to love God alone, which comes to the same thing. They find that the Messiah did not come for them. But those who are looking for God find him, without any contradiction, and find that they are commanded to love only him, and that the Messiah did come at the time foretold to bring them the blessings for which they asked.

Thus the Jews witnessed miracles and the fulfillment of prophecies. Their faith taught them to worship and to love only one God. It was a perpetual command. Therefore it possessed all the marks of true religion, which indeed it was. Yet the teaching of the Jews must be distinguished from that of the Jewish law. The teaching of the Jews was not true, in spite of having miracles, prophecies, and perpetuity, because it lacked the further precept, which was to worship and love God only. (503-675)

240. Their hearts were hardened. How? By inciting their avarice and giving them hopes of satisfying it. (496-714)

241. God used the concupiscence of the Jews so that they should be of use to Jesus Christ, who brought the remedy for such worldly lusts. (614-64)

242. God has used the blindness of this people for the benefit of his elect. (496-577)

243. Those who find it difficult to believe will seek grounds for it in the unbelief of the Jews. "If it is so clearly evidenced, then why did the Jews not believe?" they will argue. They

almost wish the Jews really had believed, so that they themselves would not have been held back by such an example of Jewish rejection. But this very refusal is the basis of our own belief. We should have been much less inclined to believe if they had been on our side. Yet the amazing thing is, that fascinated by prophecy, they were so hostile to its fulfillment. (273-745)

244. What could Messiah's enemies, the Jews, do? If they accepted him, they would have given evidence of who he was by such acceptance. It would have meant those looking for the Messiah had accepted him as such. But if they rejected him, they only showed who he was by their rejection. (262-496)

245. The Jews reject him, but not all of them; the saints accept him, but not the worldly-minded. Far from undermining his glory, this rejection is its crown and culmination. The reason they give for his rejection, and the only one found in their Scriptures, in the Talmud, and in the rabbinical writings, is merely that Jesus Christ did not use force to subdue the people. "Gird your sword upon your side, O mighty one" (Psalm 45:3). Is that all they have to say? "Jesus Christ was put to death," they declare. "He was a failure, for he did not subdue the pagans by force. He did not give us the spoils. He gave us no riches." Is that all they have to say? This is precisely why he makes us want to love him. For the kind of messiah they would envisage has no appeal to me. Clearly it is only their wickedness that prevented them from recognizing who he really is. Indeed, by their rejection they have become unimpeachable witnesses. What is more, in doing so, they are fulfilling the prophecies made concerning him.

Indeed, the very rejection of Christ enabled this very miracle to take place. For the prophecies are the only lasting miracles which can be made possible, though they are liable to be challenged. (593-760)

246. It is clear they are a people created for the express purpose of being a witness to the Messiah (Isaiah 43:9-10; 44:8). They hand down by tradition their books, loving them yet not understanding them. All this was foretold. The judgments of God were entrusted to them, but they were kept as a sealed book. (495-641)

247. If this was so clearly predicted to the Jews, why did they not believe it, or why were they not utterly destroyed for rejecting so obvious a revelation? My reply is: First, it was foretold that they would reject the truth predicted; and second, it was foretold that they would not be exterminated. Nothing is more to the glory of the Messiah than these two truths. It was not enough merely to have prophecies. They also had to be kept above suspicion. (391-749)

248. By destroying Messiah, since they would not accept him as their Messiah, the Jews actually conferred upon him this final sign that he was indeed the Messiah. By their continual rejection of him, they became unimpeachable witnesses as to who he is.

By killing him and persisting in their denial of him, they fulfilled the prophecies about him. (488-761)

XX
RABBINICAL WRITINGS

249. [Looking at the rabbinical literature itself], we have ample data to support the doctrine of original sin. Take the statement of Genesis 8:21, "Every inclination of a man's heart is evil from childhood." R. Moses Haddarschan comments: "This evil leaven is in man from the moment of his birth." *Massachet Sukkah* says: "This evil leaven has seven descriptions in Scripture: It is called evil, foreskin, uncleanness, enemy, scandal, a heart of stone, an icy blast. All represent the wickedness hidden and implanted within the heart of man." *Midrash Tehillim* says the same thing, adding that God will deliver man from his evil nature.

This wickedness of man's nature is constantly being reinforced, as it says in Psalm 37:32: "The wicked lie in wait for the righteous, seeking their very lives; but the LORD will not leave them in their power." This wickedness tries the heart of man in this life and will accuse him in the next. All this is to be found in the *Talmud*.

Midrash Tehillim makes this comment on Psalm 4:5: "Stand in awe and be fearful of evil and you will not sin." So be afraid and dread your lustful spirit, and it will not lead you into sin. Commenting on Psalm 36:1—"An oracle is within my heart concerning the sinfulness of the wicked; there is no fear of God before His eyes," it points out that the natural wickedness of man has said this about the wicked.

Midrash el Kohelet comments: "The wise but poor child is better than a foolish old king who cannot foresee the future." That is to say, the child is the virtue and the king represents the wickedness of man. It is called "king" because all the members of the body obey it, and it is "old" because it has been in the human heart from infancy to old age. It is "foolish" because it leads man into the way of destruction that he does not foresee. *Midrash Tehillim* says the same thing.

Bereshith Rabbah comments on Psalm 35:10, 11: "My whole being will exclaim, 'Who is like you, O LORD? You rescue the poor from those too strong for them, the poor and needy from those who rob them.' " Can there be a greater tyranny than such evil as the human heart? It cites Proverbs 25:21, "If your enemy is hungry, give him food to eat." That is to say, if our foul nature hungers, give it the bread of wisdom that is spoken about in Proverbs 9:4-5: " 'Let all who are simple come in here!' she says to those who lack judgment. 'Come, eat my food.' " If the soul thirsts, let it have the water that is spoken of in Isaiah 55:1: "Come, all you who are thirsty, come to the waters." *Midrash Tehillim* says the same thing, adding that the Scripture in this passage, speaking of our enemy, implies our own foul nature, and that in giving this bread and water one will heap coals of fire on his head.

Midrash el Kohelet quotes Ecclesiastes 9:14: "A powerful king came against the city, surrounded it and built huge seigeworks against it. Now there lived in that city a man poor but wise, and he saved the city by his wisdom." That is why it says in Psalm 41:1, "Blessed is he who has regard for the weak." Again in Psalm 78:39, "He remembered that they were but flesh, a passing breeze that does not return." From this some have been led into error in denying the immortality of the soul. Rather, the spirit in this context refers to the evil within a man which accompanies him until his death, but will not be restored at the resurrection. Other passages are cited: Psalm 103:16 and 16:10.

Based on such texts, rabbinic principles describe two messiahs: One who is strong and mighty and the other who is weak and wise. (278-446)

XXI
PERPETUITY, OR LASTING PRINCIPLES OF THE CHRISTIAN FAITH

250. Anyone who judges the Jewish faith by its more grossly minded adherents will misunderstand it. It can be seen from the sacred books and the tradition of the prophets that they make it clear enough that they did not interpret the law only according to the letter. So too our faith is divine both in the gospel, in the apostles and tradition, but it can be made ridiculous by those who mishandle it.

According to the worldly-minded Jews, the Messiah was to be a great temporal ruler. Likewise, according to carnal Christians, Jesus Christ came to excuse us from needing to love God and to give us sacraments that produce their effect without our help. Such is neither Christian nor Jewish faith. For true Christians, like true Jews, have always waited in expectation of a Messiah, who will cause them to love God and, by means of that love, to overcome their enemies. (287-607)

251. There are two kinds of people in every religion.

Among the pagans, there are those who worship animals and others who worship the one and only god of natural religion.

Among the Jews, there were those who were carnal, and there were those who might be called "Christians" of the old law because they were spiritually minded.

Among Christians, there are those who are grossly minded, and who may therefore be described as "the Jews" of the new law. The carnal Jews waited for a carnal Messiah, while the gross Christians believe the Messiah has dispensed them from the obligation to love God. True Jews and true Christians worship a Messiah who causes them to love God. (286-609)

252. Carnal Jews stand midway between Christians and heathen. The heathen do not know God and only love the world. The Jews know the true God, but love only the world. Jews and pagans love the same things. Jews and Christians recognize the same God.

The Jews were of two kinds: some had only heathen affections, others had Christian desires. (289-608)

253. In all religions, sincerity is essential so that we can describe people as real pagans, real Jews, and real Christians. (480-590)

254. I see the Christian faith as founded upon an earlier religion, in which I find the following facts. I am not speaking here simply about the miracles of Moses, of Jesus Christ, and of the apostles, because they do not appear at first sight to be convincing, and I do not wish to cite anything as evidence except those which are beyond doubt and which cannot be called into question by anyone. What is certain is that in various parts of the world we find a distinctive people, who are separated from all the other peoples of the world, and who are called the Jewish people.

So I see makers of religions in many parts of the world and at different times of history. But their morality fails to satisfy me, nor do their arguments convince me at all. That is why I have rejected alike the Mohammedan religion, or that of China, or that of the ancient Romans and Egyptians, simply and solely because they remain unconvincing, neither bearing the stamp of truth nor forcing me to be persuaded by them.

But as I ponder the shifting and strange variety of customs and beliefs that have existed at different periods, I find in one small corner of the world a peculiar people, set apart from all other peoples of the world, whose history is earlier by several centuries than the oldest histories we have.

So I find this great and numerous people, descended from a single man, worshiping one God, and living according to a law they claim to have received from him. They maintain they are the only people in the world to whom God has revealed his mysteries. They also claim that all men are corrupt and out of favor with God. They maintain that all have been abandoned to the influence of their senses and inclinations, and that from these proceed strange aberrations and continual uncertainties of faiths and customs among them, whereas the Jews remain unshakable in their conduct. They also maintain that God will not leave other nations forever in ignorance, for a Redeemer will come for all the world. They believe they themselves have been placed here on earth in order to proclaim him to all and are expressly created for the purposes of being the forerunners and the heralds of this great Coming, and to call all men to join with them in expectation of this Redeemer. To encounter such people amazes me, and seems to me to be worth serious attention.

As I study this law they maintain they have received from God, I find it worthy of admiration. For it is the first of all legal codes—so much so that it was used before the word *law* was in use among the Greeks—and was received and observed for nearly a thousand years without interruption. I find it remarkable that this first legal code in the world should also happen to be the most perfect, so that the greatest legislators have borrowed their own laws from it, as is evident from the twelve tables at Athens [which is pure fiction] and from other proofs put forward by Josephus.

However, the Jewish law is at the same time the most severe and most rigorous of all as regards the practice of religion. In order to bind people to their duties, it threatens them under pain of death with a great number of distinct and arduous observations. In spite of this, it is extraordinary how the law has been constantly preserved for so many centuries by a people as rebellious and impatient as they. While all other nations have from time to time altered their laws, which were far more lenient, the Jews never have. The book that contains this law is itself the oldest book in the world. Those of Homer, Hesiod, and others come only six or seven hundred years later. (451-620)

255. It is an indisputable fact that while philosophers are divided into different schools, there is found in one corner of the earth the most ancient of peoples who declare that the whole of mankind is in error. Yet God has revealed the truth to them, that it will always continue upon the earth. All other sects come to an end, but this people survives and has done so for four thousand years. They declare that this faith has been handed down from their forefathers and that man has fallen from communion with God into utter alienation from him. But God has promised to redeem mankind. This doctrine has always been taught, while their law has always had significance for their contemporary situation as well as for the future. For sixteen hundred years they had prophets they believed foretold the time and manner [of the coming of Messiah]. When they were scattered throughout the earth four hundred years later, it was because Jesus Christ was to be proclaimed universally. Their law also taught the manner in which Christ would come, and it foretold the time.

Since then the Jews have been scattered everywhere under a curse, yet they continue to survive. (456-618)

256. *Sincerity of the Jews*. Lovingly and in faithfulness they hand on this book in which Moses declares that they had all been ungrateful to God throughout all their lives, and that he knows they will be even more so after his death. He calls heaven and earth to witness against them, and has done so clearly to point out their ingratitude.

He declares that God will in the end have wrath against them and disperse them among all the peoples of the earth. For they have offended him by worshiping false gods, so he will provoke them by calling a people who are not his people in their place. God ordains that all his words will be preserved forever, and that his Book be placed in the ark of the covenant, to serve in perpetuity as a witness against them. Isaiah says the same thing (Isaiah 30:8). (452-631)

257. *The Continuity of the Faith.* The only religion that is against human nature, common sense, and man's self interest is the only one that has always existed. (284-605)

258. The only knowledge which is contrary alike to human nature and common sense is the only one always to have existed among mankind. (425-604)

259. [This biblical faith which has such continuity] consists in believing that man has fallen from a state of glory and fellowship with God into a state of despair, estrangement, and need of repentance, but that after this life we shall be restored by a promised Messiah. This has always existed. All things have passed away, but this truth, through which all things are, has endured.

In the first age of the world, men were swept into every kind of misdeed, and yet there were men of God such as Enoch, Lamech, and others who patiently waited for the Messiah promised from the beginning of the world. Noah saw human wickedness at its height, and he had the privilege to save mankind in his own person because he hoped in the Messiah, whom he foreshadowed. Abraham was surrounded by idolaters when God revealed to him the mystery of the Messiah, who he hailed from afar. In the time of Isaac and Jacob evil spread over the whole earth, but these devout men lived in their faith. Jacob, blessing his children on his deathbed, cried out in an ecstasy that interrupted his speech: "I look for Your deliverance, O LORD (Genesis 49:18).

The Egyptians were full of idolatry and magic, and even the people of God were carried away by their example. Nevertheless, Moses and others believed in God, who they had not seen, fixing their attention upon the eternal gifts he was preparing for them.

The Greeks, and afterwards the Romans, set up false gods. Their poets evolved a hundred different systems of theology, while their philosophers split up into a thousand different schools of thought. And yet in the heart of Judea, there were always chosen men who foretold the coming of that Messiah, which was revealed only to them. The Messiah himself came at length in the fullness of time, and since then we have seen so many schisms and heresies arise, so many nations overthrown, so many changes of every kind, while the church which worships him has always endured and continued without a break. What is marvelous, unique, and altogether divine is that this religion which has always survived has also always been under attack. Times without number it has been on the verge of total extinction, and every time it has been in this state God has restored her by the extraordinary intervention of his power. This is truly amazing, so the fact that she has survived without ever yielding to the will of a tyrant suggests that its laws may have to yield to necessity [but still transcend circumstances]. (281-613)

260. God willed to create for himself a holy people he would set apart from all other nations, whom he would also deliver from their enemies and bring into a place of rest. He promised to do so, foretelling by his prophets the time and manner of his coming. In order to strengthen the hope of his chosen people in every age he gave them an image of all this; he did not leave them without assurances of his power and will for their salvation. Adam, in the creation of man, was a witness to this, receiving the promise of a Savior who would be born of woman.

At a time when mankind was still so close to the creation that he could not forget his own creation and fall, yet at a time when Adam was no longer living in this world, God sent Noah, saving him and drowning the whole world by a miracle which clearly showed God's power to save the world. He expressed his will to do so and to cause to be born from the seed of woman the one he had promised.

This miracle was adequate to strengthen the hope of the elect. The memory of the flood still being so fresh among mankind while Noah was still alive, God made his promises to Abraham; and while Shem was still alive, God also sent Moses. (392-644)

261. If the early church was in error, the church today is a fallen one. But even if she should fall into error today, it would not be the same situation, for there is always the superior guidance of tradition of the faith of the early church. This submission to and conformity with the early church prevails and corrects everything. But the early church did not presuppose the future church nor consider her, as we presuppose and regard the early church. (285-867)

262. The history of the church should more accurately be called the history of truth. (776-858)

XXII
PROOFS OF MOSES

263. *Antiquity of the Jews*. What a contrast there is between one book and another! It is not surprising that the Greeks composed the *Iliad*, nor the Egyptians and Chinese their own histories. You have only to see how that came about. These historians of legend and fable were not contemporary with the things they wrote about. Homer composed a story that was offered and accepted as such. No one ever questioned that Troy and Agamemnon had never really existed, any more than the fable of the golden apple. He never meant to write a history about it, but only a diversion. He is the only distinguished writer of his times, for it is the beauty of the literary work that has enabled it to survive. Everyone learns it and discusses it. It is something that has to be known culturally and everyone learns it by heart. Four hundred years later the witnesses of these things are no longer alive. No one knows from his own experience whether the work is fable or history. It simply has to be learned from earlier generations, and that is how it passes for truth.

But any history that is not written by a contemporary is suspect. So the books of Sibylline and Trismegistus and many others that have enjoyed credibility are false and eventually have been proved to be so. But this is not the case with contemporary authors. For there is a great difference between a book composed by an individual, which he passes on to the

193

people, and a book that people compose. So there is no question that a book is as old as the people. (436-628)

264. Why does Moses represent the lives of mankind to be so long and their generations to be so few? It is not the length of years but a multitude of generations that makes things obscure. For truth is only perverted when men change. And yet the two most significant pair of events ever imagined, namely the creation and the flood, are brought so close together that we seem to be able to touch them both. (292-624)

265. *Another Circle.* The longevity of the patriarchs, instead of causing the history of past events to be lost in obscurity, serve on the contrary to keep it. We are sometimes not well-informed about the history of our predecessors because we have barely lived with them for any length of time, and they are often dead before we have reached the age of reason. So, when men lived to a very great age, their children lived for a long time with their parents. They conversed with them over a prolonged period. And what else would they have talked about but the history of their ancestors? That was all that history really amounted to. They had no studies nor sciences nor art, which serve today to be a major part of the conversations of our daily life. We also find that people at that time took particular care to preserve their genealogies. (290-626)

266. Shem, who saw Lamech, who saw Adam, also saw Jacob, who saw those who saw Moses. [With such continuity] that is why the stories of the flood and creation are true. This evidence is conclusive among certain people who really understand the matter. (296-625)

267. When the event of the creation of the world began to recede into the past, a remarkable contemporary historian was provided by God, and entrusted an entire people with the keeping of this book, so that this should be the most

authentic history in the world. Then all men could learn from it something which was vital for them to know and which could only be known from it. (474-622)

268. When the creation and flood had taken place, God pledged not only that he would never again destroy the world in this fashion, but that he was going to reveal himself in spectacular ways. He began to establish a people upon the earth, especially created, who were to continue until the Messiah would create a people through his own Spirit. (435-621)

269. As long as the prophets were there to maintain the law, the people paid no attention to it; but once there were no more prophets, zeal took their place. (294-703)

270. The zeal of the Jewish people for their law [was remarkable], especially since there had been no more prophets. (297-702)

XXIII
PROOFS OF JESUS CHRIST

271. [We come now to] Jesus Christ, with whom both Testaments are concerned. The Old Testament focus is on expectation while the focus of the New is on realization. But Jesus is at the center of them both. (388-740)

272. Only Jesus Christ could create a great people, elect them to be holy and chosen, lead them, feed them, and bring them into the place of rest and holiness. He alone could make them holy for God, the temple of God, by reconciling them with God and saving them from God's anger. Only he could redeem them from the bondage of sin which so obviously dominates mankind, giving laws to this people, and writing them in their hearts. Only he could offer himself to God on their behalf, sacrifice himself for them as a perfect offering, and be himself the High Priest offering up his body and blood, yet in worship offering up bread and wine to God. As Hebrews 10:5 sums it up: "When he comes into the world . . ." Again the reference is made in Mark 13:2 that when the physical temple is utterly destroyed there is not "one stone upon another." Then what came before will continue afterwards. Compared with Jesus Christ the Jews simply survive as wanderers. (608-766)

273. Numerous prophecies are made concerning the Messiah: A riddle (Ezekiel 17); his precursor (Malachi 3); he would be

born as a child (Isaiah 9); he would be born in the town of Bethlehem (Micah 5); he would appear mainly in Jerusalem, and be born of the family of Judah and David. It is prophesied about him that he would be the one to blind the wise and learned (Isaiah 6, 8-29, 61). He would preach good tidings to the poor and the meek, open the eyes of the blind, heal the sick, and lead those who languished in darkness into the light (Isaiah 61). He is predicted as the One to teach the way of perfection and be the Teacher of the Gentiles (Isaiah 56; 42:1-7).

Indeed, the prophecies are unintelligible to the godless (Daniel 12; Hosea 14:9). But they would be understood by those who were properly instructed in them. The prophecies represent Messiah as poor, and yet see him ruling the nations (Isaiah 52:13-53:12; Zechariah 9:9). The prophecies that predict the time of his coming speak of him as the ruler of the Gentiles and yet One who suffers, not coming transcendently in the clouds and as a Judge. Those prophecies which speak of him as a Judge and of his glory, do not specify the time. They also describe him as the victim for the sins of the world (Isaiah 49, 53).

He is prophesied to be the precious cornerstone (Isaiah 28:16). He is to be the stone of stumbling and the rock of offense (Isaiah 8). Jerusalem is to destroy itself against this stone. The builders are to reject it (Psalm 118:22). Yet God is to make this stone the head of the corner. It is to grow into a great mountain that fills all the earth (Daniel 2). But the prophecies also speak of his rejection, unrecognition, and betrayal (Psalm 109). It is predicted that he would be sold in treachery (Zechariah 11:12). They would spit upon him, strike him and mock him, afflicting him in countless ways, and give him gall to drink (Psalm 69:21). His body is to be pierced (Zechariah 12:10), his hands and his feet nailed. He is to be slain. Lots are to be cast for his garment (Psalm 22).

Yet he is to rise again the third day (Psalm 16; Hosea 6:2). He would ascend into heaven to sit on the right hand of God (Psalm 110). It is predicted that kings would take up arms against him (Psalm 2). Being victorious over his enemies he would be set on the right hand of the Father. Kings of the

earth and all peoples will worship him (Isaiah 60). The Jews
will continue to exist as a nation (Jeremiah). They will be
without kings as wanderers (Hosea 3) and without prophets
(Amos), awaiting salvation and yet not finding it (Isaiah).
The Gentiles would be called through Jesus Christ (Isaiah
52:15; 55-60; Psalm 72:8-17). Hosea 1:9-10 prophesies: "Call
him Lo-Ammi, for you are not my people, and I am not your
God. . . . In the place where it was said to them, 'You are not
my people,' they will be called 'sons of the living God.' "
(487-727)

274. Moses first teaches the Trinity, original sin, and the
Messiah. David is a great witness: He is a kind, good,
merciful, noble soul, powerful, and with a lofty mind. He
prophesies and it comes to pass. This is infinite. If he had
been full of vanity, he might have proclaimed himself to be
the Messiah, for the prophecies were clearer about himself
than about Jesus Christ. The same is also true of the apostle
John. (315-752)

275. The synagogue came before the church, as the Jews
before the Christians. But the prophets foretold the
Christians; the apostle John, Jesus Christ. (319-699)

276. The zeal of the Jews for their law and temple is evidenced in the writings of Josephus and Philo the Jew. What
other people have had such zeal? It was necessary, perhaps,
that they should have it.

Jesus foretold the times and the state of the world. Genesis
49:10 describes him as "the ruler's staff" and Daniel 2:40
speaks of "the fourth monarchy." How fortunate we are to
possess this light amidst such obscurity! How good it is to see
with the eyes of faith Darius and Cyrus, Alexander, the
Romans, Pompey, and Herod, all contributing, though
unconsciously, to the glory of the gospel! (317-701)

277. When the Jews in captivity had the assurance of being
released within seventy years, it was no real captivity. But
now they are captive and without hope. God promised them

that even though he should scatter them to the ends of the earth, yet, if they remained faithful to his law, he would bring them together again. Still oppressed, they remained faithful to it. (305-638)

278. When Nebuchadnezzar carried away the people captive, in case they thought the scepter had been forever removed from Judah, God told them beforehand that their captivity would not last long, and that they would be restored (Jeremiah 29:10). They were comforted throughout by the prophets, and their royal house continued. But the second destruction came without any promise of restoration— without having prophets, without kings, without consolation and hope, because the scepter has forever been removed. (314-639)

279. It is truly amazing and remarkable to see how this Jewish people has survived for so many centuries and yet always so unfortunate. Yet this is necessary as a proof of Jesus Christ, that they should survive to demonstrate who he is and still to be in their wretched condition, since they crucified him. And although it is a paradox that they should both survive and yet be wretched, they still survive despite their misfortunes. (311-640)

280. *The Gospel Portrait.* There appear to be apparent discrepancies between the Gospels. (318-755)

281. Who taught the Evangelists the qualities of a supremely heroic soul, so that they could depict one so perfectly in Jesus Christ? Yet, why then do we show him as weak in his agony? Do they not know how to depict a resolute death? Yes indeed, for the same Luke himself describes the death of Stephen more heroically than that of Jesus Christ (Acts 7:58).

They make him as capable of fear, before the inevitability of death arises, and then absolutely steadfast. But when they show him so distressed, it is when he afflicts himself. But when men afflict him he is absolutely steadfast. (316-800)

282. The apostles were either deceived or were deceivers. Both suppositions are fraught with difficulty, for it is not possible to mistake a man risen from the dead.

So long as Jesus Christ was with them, he could sustain them. But afterwards, if he did not appear to them, who then inspired their actions? (322-802)

283. The hypothesis that the apostles were impostors is quite absurd. Let us examine this critically and just imagine the twelve men gathered together after the death of Jesus Christ, conspiring to say that he had risen from the dead. In doing so they attack all the powers that be. Now, since the human heart is singularly susceptible to fickleness, to change, to promises, and to bribery, consider the consequences. However little one of the Twelve had been misguided to deny his story under these inducements, or still more had been terrorized by the possible threat of imprisonment, torture and death, they would all have been lost. So follow that out to its logical conclusion. (310-801)

284. The style of the Gospels is remarkable in many ways. One characteristic of them is that they never heap invective against the executioners and enemies of Christ. None of them as historians writes against Judas, Pilate, or indeed any of the Jews.

If this restraint of the Evangelists had been make-belief, together with so many other noble characteristics of their style, and if they had only put it on in pretense to draw attention, not daring to remark on it themselves, they would not have failed to make friends for their own benefit from such remarks. But since they acted with integrity and without any self-interest, they did not cause anyone to remark on this. And I believe many of these things have never been remarked on before. That only shows how detached was the way they acted. (812-798)

285. Anyone can do what Mohammed did. He performed no miracles and was not foretold. No one can do what Jesus Christ did. (598-600)

286. A laborer who speaks of wealth, a lawyer who speaks of war, or of kingship, etc., [will speak inappropriately]. But the rich man rightly speaks of wealth, the king can speak indifferently of a great gift he has just made, and so God rightly speaks of God. (303-799)

287. Jesus Christ says sublime things so simply that it seems as though he has not prayerfully considered them, ánd yet so clearly that we see exactly what he thought about them. This combination of clarity with such simplicity is marvelous. (309-797)

288. The church has had as much difficulty in demonstrating that Jesus Christ was man, against those who denied it, as in proving that he was God; yet both were equally evident. (307-764).

289. *The Obscurity of Jesus Christ.* Jesus Christ is in such obscurity (according to what the world conceives obscurity to be) that historians, writing only of important affairs of state, hardly noticed him. (300-786)

290. What human being ever had greater glory? The entire Jewish nation foretells him before his coming, while the Gentiles worship him after his advent. Both the Jewish and the Gentile peoples regarded him as their focus.

Yet what man ever enjoyed such glory least of all? For thirty of his thirty-three years he lives a hidden life. And for three years he is treated as an impostor. The priests and rulers reject him. Those who are closest and dearest to him despise him. Finally he died betrayed by one of his disciples, is denied by another, and is forsaken by all.

What benefit, then, did he derive from such glory? No one ever had greater glory, yet no man ever suffered greater shame. All of this glory has only been to our benefit, to help us to recognize him, for he took none of it for himself. (499-792)

291. The infinite distance between the mind and the body is a symbol of the distance that is infinitely more, between the intellect and love, for love is divine.

All the splendor of greatness has no luster for those who are engaged in scholarly pursuits. The greatness of scholars is invisible to kings, to rich men, to military leaders, to all who are great in a worldly sense.

The greatness of wisdom, which is nothing unless it comes from God, is not seen by the worldly minded or by intellectual people. They represent three distinct orders that differ in character.

Great geniuses have their dominion, their splendor, their greatness, their victory, their reputation, and have no need of worldly standing, with which they have no affinity. For they are not outwardly visible, but only to the mind and that is enough. Likewise, saints have their dominion, their brilliance, their victory, their luster, and they, too, neither need worldly or intellectual greatness which has no relevance for them, for it neither increases or diminishes their own stature. For God and the angelic hosts recognize them, but not by bodies or curious minds. God is enough for them.

Archimedes, though in obscurity, still commanded respect. He fought no battles visible to the human eye, yet he enriched every mind with his discoveries. How brightly he shone in the minds of men!

Jesus Christ, without wealth and without any outward show of knowledge, occupies his own standing in holiness. He made no discoveries. He did not rule, but was humble, patient, holy, holy, holy to God, terrible to devils, and without sin. O, in what great pomp and marvelous glory he reveals himself to the eyes of the heart that perceive wisdom indeed!

It would have been useless of Archimedes to play the role of the prince in his mathematical works, though indeed he was a prince. Likewise, it would have been useless for our Lord Jesus Christ to come as a king with the kind of glory inappropriate to his purpose. So it is quite absurd to be scandalized by the lowliness of Jesus Christ, as if that lowliness was of the same order as is the greatness he came to reveal. For if we consider his greatness in life, his passion, his obscurity, and his death, the way he chose his disciples, in their abandonment of him, in his secret resurrection and the rest, we shall have no cause to be shocked by the lowliness which is not of that order.

But there are some who are only capable of admiring worldly greatness, as though there were no such thing as intellectual eminence, or as if there were no infinitely higher forms of greatness in the realm of wisdom. All bodies, the universe, the stars, the earth and its kingdoms are not equal to the least of the minds, for it knows them all and itself too, while bodies know nothing. So all bodies put together and all minds, with all their products, are unworthy to be equaled to the least motion of love, which belongs to an infinitely superior order of things. One will never succeed in obtaining a single small thought from all the bodies put together. That is quite impossible, since thought belongs to a different dimension. One cannot produce any feeling of true love from the combination of all bodies and minds. That too is impossible, for love belongs to a different, supernatural dimension. (308-793)

292. *Against the objection the Scripture has no order.* The heart has its own order, the mind has its own, which uses principles and demonstrations. The heart has a different one. So our claim to be loved cannot be proved by setting out in order the causes of love; that would be absurd.

Jesus Christ and St. Paul employ the method of love, not of the intellect. They sought to humble, not to instruct. Likewise with St. Augustine. This method consists primarily in digressing from every point that relates to the end, so that this is always kept in sight. (298-283)

XXIV
PROPHECIES OF SCRIPTURE

293. The climax of all that was foretold was to demonstrate that it could not be said it was all due to chance.

Anyone with only a week to live is not interested in believing that all this is merely the work of chance.

Now, if the passions had no hold upon us, whether we had a week or a hundred years would amount to the same thing. (326-694)

294. But it was not just that there had to be prophecies. They had to be communicated throughout the world and preserved through every generation. In that way it could not be thought that by mere chance Messiah's coming just happened to be foretold. So indeed it was much more to the glory of the Messiah that the Jews should be spectators, even the instruments of his glory, apart from the fact that God had purposed this for them. (385-707)

295. The prophecies are the strongest proofs of Jesus Christ. It is for them that God made most abundant evidence, for the event which fulfilled them is a miracle that endures from beginning until the end of the church. For this purpose God raised up prophets over a period of some sixteen hundred years, and then during a period of four hundred years scattered the prophecies with the diaspora of the Jews,

carrying them into every corner of the earth. Such was the preparation for the birth of Jesus Christ. Since his gospel had to be believed by the whole world, it was necessary that not only should there be such prophecies to create such belief, but that these prophecies should be spread throughout the world so that the whole world might embrace it. (335-706)

296. One can only stand in awe of a man who clearly foretells things that come to pass, and who declares his intention of both illuminating and blinding, and who mixes in obscurity with clear things that come to pass. (344-756)

297. If one man alone had written a book of prophecies about Jesus Christ, concerning the time and manner of his advent, and if Jesus Christ had come in accordance with these prophecies, this would carry great weight.

But there is far more to it than this. For some four thousand years, a succession of men followed each other and consistently and invariably predicted the same advent. A whole people proclaimed it and existed for some four thousand years in order to bear corporate witness of the assurances they had received and which they could not forget, no matter what threats and persecutions they were called upon to suffer. This is much more impressive. (332-710)

298. Thus for sixteen hundred years they had men they believed to be prophets foretelling the manner and time of his advent.

Four hundred years later they were scattered everywhere, because Jesus Christ had to be proclaimed everywhere. Then Jesus Christ came in the way and at the time. Since then, the Jews have been scattered everywhere as a curse, and yet still survive as a people. (456-618)

299. It takes courage to foretell the same thing in so many different ways. The four monarchies, idolatrous or pagan, the end of the reign of Judah, and the seventy weeks, all had to take place at the same time and before the second temple was destroyed. (336-709)

300. The little stone of Daniel 2:35 implies that Jesus would be small in his beginning but grow afterward. If I had never heard anything at all about the Messiah, yet after seeing the fulfillment of such wonderful prophecies about the events of the world, I would see that this is truly of God. And if I knew these same books foretold a Messiah, I would feel assured that he would surely come, and seeing that they had put the time before the destruction of the second temple, I would be confident to say that he had indeed come. (329-734)

301. After many prophets had gone before him, Jesus Christ finally came to say: "Here I am, now is the time. What the prophets said was to happen in the fullness of time, I tell you my apostles will accomplish. The Jews will be cast out. Jerusalem will soon be destroyed. The heathen will enter into the knowledge of God. My apostles will accomplish this after you have slain the heir to the vineyard" (Mark 12:8).

Then the apostles said to the Jews: "You shall be accursed" (although Celsus laughed at this). And they told the heathen: "You shall enter into the knowledge of God," and this came to pass. (327-770)

302. It was foretold that at the time of the advent of the Messiah, he would establish a new covenant that would make them forget how they came out of Egypt (Jeremiah 23:7; Isaiah 43:16). It was also predicted that he would set his law not in outward things but within their hearts; and that he would implant the fear of the Lord, which had never been more than in outward things, into their innermost hearts. Who cannot fail to see the Christian law in all this? (346-729)

303. It was predicted that the Jews would reject Jesus Christ and would be rejected by God because the chosen vine had brought forth only sour grapes. It was also predicted that the chosen people would be unfaithful, ungrateful, and unbelieving (Romans 10:21; see Isaiah 65:2). They were described as "a disobedient and obstinate people."

It was also predicted that God would smite them with blindness, so that they would grope at noonday like the blind. It was also predicted that a forerunner would come before him to prepare his way (Malachi 3:1). (347-735)

304. Since subsequent events have proved that these prophecies were divinely inspired, the rest of them ought to be believed; thus we can see the order of the world in this way.

When the miracles of creation and the flood were overlooked, God then sent the law and the miracles of Moses and the prophets who prophesied certain things. Then in order to prepare a lasting miracle God prepared prophecies and their fulfillment. Then since the prophecies themselves might be suspect, he desired to put them above all question. (594-576)

305. Therefore I reject all other religions, and I find an answer to all objections. It is reasonable that so holy a God should disclose himself only to those whose hearts are sanctified. Therefore this religion attracts people, and I find it wholly convincing by so divine a morality, but I find more in it than that. I find that as far back as human memory can go, there is listed a people more ancient than any other. Men have constantly been told they are totally corrupt, but a Redeemer would come. It was not just one man who said this but countless people, and indeed a whole nation, who prophesied this explicitly for four thousand years. Their books were scattered for four hundred years.

The more I look into the matter the more truth I find. A whole people predicts his advent, and a whole people worship him after his advent. What went before also came after. The synagogue which went before him, a number of wretched Jews without prophets came after him. Those all being hostile were yet admirable witnesses of the truth of the prophecies which foretold their blindness and wretchedness. Finally, the Jews are without idols or king.

The fearful darkness of the Jews was foretold: "At midday you will grope about like a blind man in the dark. You will be unsuccessful in everything you do; day after day you will be oppressed and robbed, with no one to rescue you" (Deuteronomy 28:29). It was also foretold: "For you this whole vision is nothing but words sealed in a scroll. And if you give the scroll to someone who can read, and say to him, 'Read this, please,' he will answer, 'I can't; it is sealed.' Or if you give the scroll to someone who cannot read and say, 'Read this, please,' he will answer, 'I don't know how to read'" (Isaiah 29:11-12).

While the scepter is still in the hands of the first foreign usurper, there is this rumor of Christ's advent. How I marvel at this original and inspiring faith, wholly divine in its authority, its continuance, its antiquity, its morality, its conduct, its doctrine, and in its effects.

So I stretch out my hands to my Savior, who having been foretold for some four thousand years, came to earth to die and suffer for me in the time and circumstances foretold. By his grace I await even death in tranquility, in the hope of being eternally united to him. Meanwhile I live full of joy, with the blessings he has been pleased to bestow upon me or in the afflictions he will send for my own good and which he teaches me how to endure by faith's example. (593-737)

XXV
PARTICULAR FIGURES OF PROPHECY

306. The twofold law, the two tables of the law, the twofold temple, the twofold captivity. (349-652)

307. Japheth begins the genealogy. Jacob crosses his arms, and chooses the younger son. (350-623)

308. The Jews were still strangers in Egypt, without possessions of their own, either in that land or anywhere else. (Nor was there the slightest hint of kingship among them, which came long after, nor of a supreme council of seventy judges, which they called "the Sanhedrin," which was set up by Moses, and continued until the time of Christ. All these institutions were as far removed from the original circumstances of the Jews as they could have been imagined.) For originally, from his deathbed, Jacob blessed his twelve sons and told them they would inherit a great land, and foretold in particular that from the family of Judah, kings would one day rule over all the brothers of his own race. (Even the Messiah, the hope of all peoples, would arise from his family line, and the kingship would not be taken from Judah, nor the ruler and lawgiver from his descendants, until the Messiah was born into his family.)

Jacob, disposing of that future land (as if he were already its owner), gave Joseph a portion more than he gave to the others. "I give you," he said, "one share more than to the others." Then, when he came to bless the two sons, Ephraim and Manasseh, whom Joseph had presented to him, with Manasseh the elder one on his right and Ephraim the younger one on his left, he crossed his arms and blessed them accordingly. When Joseph pointed out that he was giving preference to the younger, he answered with marked conviction: "I know my son, I realize perfectly well, but Ephraim will increase much more so than Manasseh." So true did this turn out to be that, being alone almost as fruitful as the two family lines together that made up the whole kingdom, those lines were generally called by the single name of Ephraim (see Genesis 48:22).

The same Joseph, when he lay dying, charged his children to carry his bones with them until they entered the land, which they did only after they got there some two hundred years later.

Moses, who wrote down all these things so long after they happened, assigned to each family its share of the land before they even got there, as if he was already in possession of it. Then he finally declared that God would raise up from their nation and their people a prophet whom he prefigured. He foretold exactly how they would fare in the land they would enter after his death, the victories God would give them, their ingratitude to God, the punishments they would suffer in consequence, and the rest of their adventures.

God gave them judges who would divide the land. He prescribed the whole framework of government they should observe, the cities of refuge they should build, and much else. (484-711)

309. *Christ prefigured by Joseph.* Innocent, beloved of his father, commissioned by his father to meet his brethren, he was sold for twenty pieces of silver by his brothers. Yet it was through this that he became their master and savior, savior of strangers and indeed of the world. None of this would have happened had there not been the plot to sell him, destroy him, and to totally reject him.

In prison Joseph lay innocent between two criminals. Jesus likewise lay on the cross between two thieves. He foretells the salvation of one and the death of the other, when to all appearances they were just the same. Christ saves the elect and condemns the reprobate for the same crime. But whereas Joseph only prophesies, Jesus acts. Joseph asks the man who will be saved to remember him when he is elevated. But Jesus saves the man who asks that he be remembered when Jesus comes into his kingdom. (570-768)

XXVI
CHRISTIAN MORALITY

310. Reflect on the wretchedness of man without God. The happiness of man with God. (6-60)

311. None is so happy as a true Christian, none so reasonable, so virtuous, or so lovable. (357-541)

312. Only Christianity makes men both happy and lovable. Whereas the honor of a gentleman does not permit him to be both happy and lovable. (426-542)

313. The God of the Christians is a God who makes the soul aware that he is its only good. In him alone it can find peace. Only in loving him can it find joy. He is a God who at the same time fills the soul with loathing for those things that hold it back and thus prevent it from loving God with all its might. Self-love and lust, which keep it back, are intolerable. So God makes the soul aware of this underlying self-love which destroys it. He alone can cure it. (460-544)

314. We must only love God, and we must only hate ourselves. (373a-476a)

315. These two laws are enough to rule the whole Christian republic better than all political laws. (376-484)

316. If God exists we must love him alone and not creatures that will pass away. The argument of the godless in wisdom is founded solely on the assumption that God does not exist. "Granted that," they argue, "let us then rejoice in creatures." But this is second-best. For if there were a God to love, they would not have come to this conclusion, but quite the opposite. And this is what the wise conclude: "God exists, so let us not rejoice in creatures."

Everything that entices us to become attached to creatures is bad, since it keeps us from serving God, if we know him, or from seeking him if we do not. As we are full of lusts, therefore we are full of evil, and therefore we ought to hate ourselves and all things which seduce us to become attached to anything but God alone. (618-479)

317. Experience demonstrates the great difference between piety and goodness. (365-496)

318. Of all the things upon the earth, man shares only the pains and not the pleasures. He loves those things which are near to him, but his charity does not keep these within bounds, but extends beyond to his enemies, and then to God's enemies. (355-767)

319. To control the love that we owe to ourselves, we must imagine a body full of thinking members (for we are members of the whole), and see how each member ought to love itself. (368-474)

320. When God created the heavens and the earth, which are not conscious of the bliss of their existence, he desired to create beings who would realize it and compose a body of thinking members. For our own members are unconscious of the happiness of their union, their wonderful understanding, the care taken by nature to infuse them with spirits and to enable them to grow and have fortitude. How happy they would be if they could feel and recognize all this. But in order to have this they would need to have intelligence to

know it and the good will that would confirm with that of the overall divine will. If, when they had been given intelligence, they used it in order to nourish themselves without sharing it with the other members, they would not only be wrong but miserable, hating rather than loving themselves, for their delight as much as their duty consists in consenting to the well-being of the whole soul to which they belong, which loves them better than they love themselves. (360-482)

321. To make sure that the members are happy, they must have a will and allow it conform to the body. (370-480)

322. To be a member is to have no life, no existence, and no movement except through the spirit of the whole body and for the body. A separated member that no longer recognizes the whole body to which it belongs is only a wasting and cancerous thing. It assumes it is part of the whole, but seeing no body on which it depends, believes it is dependent only on itself and so makes it the focus of its own existence. Yet not having in itself any source of life, it can only wander about and become bewildered at the uncertainty of its own existence, conscious that it is not the body and yet not recognizing that it is a member of a body. The result is that when it comes to recognize itself, it returns home as it were and only loves itself for the sake of the whole body. It will then deplore its past waywardness.

It cannot by its very being love anything else except for selfish reasons and in order to enslave itself, because each thing loves itself more than anything else.

But in loving the body it loves itself, because it has not being except in the body, for the purpose of the body and through the body. "But he that is joined unto the Lord is one spirit" (1 Corinthians 6:17).

The body loves the hand, and if it had a will the hand ought to love itself in the same way as the soul does. Any love that goes beyond that is wrong.

"He that is joined to the Lord is one spirit." That is to say, we love ourselves because we are members of Christ. We love

Christ because he is the body of which we are members. All are one. One is in the other like the three persons of the Trinity. (372-483)

323. If the foot had never realized it belonged to the body, and that there was a body on which it depended, if it had only known and loved itself and then came to know that it really belonged to the body on which it depended, think of the regret and shame it would feel for its past existence. It would recognize how useless it had been to the body in spite of the life poured into it, and how it would have been destroyed if the body had rejected it and cut it off as the foot cut itself off from the body! How it would have desired earnestly to be kept on! How obediently it would let itself be governed by the will in charge of the body, to the point of being amputated if necessary! Otherwise it would cease to be a member, for every member must be ready to perish for the sake of the whole, for whose sake alone everything exists. (373b-476)

324. The example of noble deaths such as the Spartans and others hardly move us, for we do not see what good it is to us. But the example of the deaths of Christian martyrs move us, for they are our members, having a common bond with them, so that their devotion inspires us not only by their example, but because we should have the same.

There is none of this motivation in heathen examples, for we have no links with them, just as we do not become rich by seeing a rich stranger, but rather being inspired by a father or husband who is rich. (359-481)

325. There are two kinds of men in every religion: those who are superstitious, and those who are lustful. (330-366)

326. It is mere superstition to place one's hope in formalities; but it is pride to refuse to submit to them. (364-249)

327. We must integrate what is outward with that which is inward in order to receive anything from God. In other

words, we must get down on our knees, and then pray with our lips, so that the proud man who will not submit to God must now submit to God's creature. If we merely expect help from an outward show, we are being superstitious. If we refuse to combine it with the inward, we show that we are arrogant. (944-250)

328. Christianity is strange. It orders man to acknowledge that he is evil, even abominable. Yet it also bids him to desire to be like God. Without such a counterpoise, this dignity would make him horribly vain, or promote such humiliation that would make him terribly abject. (351-537)

329. How little pride the Christian feels in being at one in union with God! With how little humility he likens himself to the earthworm! What a fine way to meet life and death, good and evil! (358-538)

330. Christian morality consists neither of a degree of abasement that we consider renders us incapable of good, nor a degree of holiness that we think is free from evil. (353-529)

331. There is no doctrine better suited to man than that which teaches him his twofold capacity both to receive and to forfeit grace, on account of the twin peril—despair and pride—to which he is always exposed. (354-524)

332. Misery leads to despair.
   Pride leads to presumption.
   The Incarnation reveals to man the enormity of his misery through the greatness of the remedy it requires. (352-526)

333. The Scriptures provide us with passages to bring comfort to every situation, and yet to have fear in every situation. Nature seems to have done the same thing through two natural, moral infinities. For we always shall have what is both higher and lower, what is more able and less able, what is more glorious and more miserable, to humble our pride and to raise us in our abasement. (800-532)

334. "Everything in the world—the cravings of sinful man, the lust of his eyes and the boasting of what he has and does—comes not from the Father but from the world" (1 John 2:16). How miserable is that cursed sphere that is consumed rather than watered by these three streams of fire! Happy are those who are beside those rivers, neither inundated nor swept away, but immovably rooted beside these streams, not standing but sitting in a humble and safe place. They will not arrogantly exalt themselves above the light, but resting in peace, stretch out their hands to him who will exalt them to stand upright and resolute in the porches of Jerusalem, the sphere of the blessed, where pride shall no longer be able to contest against them and lay them low. Yet they weep, not merely at the sight of all the perishable things swept away by these floods, but at the memory of their dearest home, the heavenly Jerusalem. This they constantly remember throughout the long years of their exile. (545-458)

XXVII
CONCLUSION

Conversion

335. The evidences for the Christian faith are as follows:

1. It establishes itself so firmly and yet so gently, although it is so contrasted to the natural life of man;
2. The holiness, sublimity, and humility of a Christian soul;
3. The miracles of Holy Scripture;
4. Jesus Christ in particular;
5. The apostles in particular;
6. Moses and the prophets in particular;
7. The Jewish people;
8. Prophecies;
9. Its continuity—no religion enjoys such perpetuity;
10. The doctrines of faith that account for everything;
11. The holiness of the law;
12. By the evidence of the order of the world.

Without any hesitation after reflecting upon these evidences, as we consider it the nature of life and of the Christian faith, we ought not to resist the inclination to follow it if our hearts are so inclined. Certainly, there are no grounds for mocking at those who do follow it. (482-289)

336. The prophecies of Scripture, even the miracles and proofs of our faith, are not the kind of evidence that are

absolutely convincing. At the same time it is not unreasonable to believe in them. There is thus evidence and obscurity, to enlighten some and confuse others. But the evidence is such as to exceed, or at least balance, the contrary evidence, so that it is not reason that decides us against following the faith. Therefore the only things that keep us from accepting the evidence must be lust and the wickedness of heart. There is therefore enough evidence to condemn and yet not enough to convince, so that it is obvious that those who follow it are prompted to do so by grace and not by reason. Those who evade its message are induced to do so by lust and not by reason.

"Really disciples" (John 8:31). "Really an Israelite" (John 1:47). "Really free" (John 8:36). "Really meat" (John 6:55). I presume that one does believe in miracles. (835-564).

337. [According to the *Summa Theologica* of Thomas Aquinas] "miracles do not serve to convert, but to condemn." (379-825)

338. He argues "a miracle would not strengthen my faith." He says this when he sees none.

There are reasons which, when seen from a distance, seem to limit our vision. But when we get close up, we begin to see beyond them. For nothing checks the ready flow of our minds. There is no rule, we argue, to which there is no exception, nor any truth that is so general that it does not present some defective aspect. It is enough for it not to be absolutely universal, to give us excuse for applying the exception to the subject at hand, and to say, "This is not always true. Therefore there are cases where it does not exist." It only remains to show that this is one of them, and we shall be very clumsy or unfortunate if we cannot find some loophole. (574-263)

339. Eloquence is a depiction of thought. So those who add still more to the original painting are producing a picture rather than a portrait. (578-344)

340. Our faith is both wise and foolish. It is wise because it is the most learned and most strongly based upon miracles, prophecies, and so on. But it is foolish because it is not for these reasons that people adhere to it. This is reason enough to condemn those who do not belong, but it is not for making those who do belong believe in it. What makes them believe is the cross. "Lest the cross of Christ be emptied of its power" (1 Corinthians 1:17).

Thus the apostle Paul, who came with signs and wisdom, affirmed that he came neither with signs or wisdom, for he came to convert. Those who come only to convince are the ones who affirm that they come with signs and wisdom. (842-588)

Faith

341. Faith is a gift of God. So do not imagine that it can be described as a gift of reason. Other religions do not make this claim for their faith. Instead they offer nothing but reason as a way of faith, and yet it does not lead there. (588-379)

342. Faith is different from truth. The one is a gift of God and the other is human. "The righteous will live by faith" (Romans 1:17). This is the faith God himself puts into our hearts, although he often uses proof as the instrument. "Faith comes from hearing the message" (Romans 10:17). But this faith dwells in our hearts, and helps us to say not "I know," but "I believe." (7-248)

343. Do not be surprised to find simple people believing without argument. For God makes them love him and hate themselves. He inclines their hearts to believe. We shall never believe with an effective belief and faith unless God inclines our hearts. Then we shall believe as soon as he inclines them. And that is what David experienced so deeply: "Turn my heart toward your statues and not toward selfish gain" (Psalm 119:36). (380-825)

344. Those who believe without having read the testaments do so because they have an inward disposition toward what is

truly holy, and because all that they hear about our faith is attractive to them. They feel that a God has created them, whom they only want to love, and therefore only desire to hate themselves. They feel they have no strength in themselves. They are incapable at the same time of coming to God. And if God does not come to them, they are unable to have any fellowship with him. Moreover, they are convinced by our faith that men must love God alone and hate only themselves. But since all men are corrupt and unworthy of God, God himself became man in order to unite himself with us. This is enough to convince them, since their hearts are so disposed, and who have this knowledge of their duty and yet of their own insufficiency. (381-286)

345. Those we see to be Christians without knowledge of the prophecies and such evidences nevertheless judge of their faith quite as well as those who possess such knowledge. They judge with their hearts, whereas others judge with their minds. For it is God himself who inclines them to believe, and thus they are most effectively convinced.

It may be argued that this way of judging is unreliable, and that it is by following such a method that heretics and unbelievers go astray.

To that my answer is that God genuinely inclines those he loves to believe in the Christian faith, and that unbelievers have no proof of what they say. But those who know the proofs of faith will prove without difficulty that such a believer is truly inspired of God, although he himself cannot prove it. For since God has declared by his prophets that in the reign of Jesus Christ he would send his Spirit abroad among the nations, so that youths and maidens and children of the church would prophesy, so it is likewise certain that the Spirit of God is upon these and not upon others. Of those he loves, God inclines their hearts (Psalm 119:36). (382-287)

Discipline

346. What a vast difference there is between the acknowledgment of, and the experience of, the love of God! (377-280)

347. People often mistake their imagination for their heart, and so often are convinced they are converted as soon as they start thinking of becoming converted. (975-275)

348. We must not misunderstand ourselves. We are as much machines as mind. As a result, the way in which persuasion is effected is not merely by demonstration. Indeed, how few things are demonstrated! Proofs only convince the mind. Our strongest proofs and those most generally accepted with conviction are those created by habit. So it is habit that guides the automaton, which leads the mind mechanically or unconsciously along. Whoever proved that it will dawn tomorrow, and that we shall die? And yet what is more widely accepted?

It is clear, then, that habit persuades us of the fact. It is habit that makes the majority of Christians, just as it does to Turks or heathen, workers, soldiers, and so on. The faith received at baptism is the advantage Christians have over the pagan world. In short, we must appeal to faith when once the mind has seen where truth resides, in order to quench our thirst and to absorb that belief which forever eludes our grasp. For it is difficult to have proofs always at hand. So we must acquire an easier belief, namely that which is conveyed by habit, which gently, simply, and intuitively nurtures belief, and so inclines all our faculties and powers so that our soul naturally accepts it. It is not good enough when belief has to be impelled by conviction, while the automaton is still inclined to believe the opposite. We must therefore take both parts of our nature and integrate them into one belief; the mind by reasons which suffice it to see once in a lifetime, and the machine by habit, not allowing it to incline to the contrary. "Incline my heart, O God" (Psalm 119:36).

The mind works slowly, looking so frequently at many differing principles which must always be considered together. So it is constantly nodding or straying because all its principles are not there present. Feeling does not work like that, but works immediately, and is always alert. So we must put our faith into our feeling, or else it will always be vacillating. (821-252)

349. There are three ways to belief: reason, habit, revelation. The Christian faith, which alone has reason, does not admit as her true children those who reject revelation. It is not that it excludes reason and habit, quite the contrary, but the mind must be habitually open to proofs and must humble itself to bow to revelation as the only true and salutary influence. "Lest the cross of Christ be emptied of its power"(1 Corinthians 1:17). (808-245)

OTHER MAXIMS
FROM THE
PENSÉES AND THE SAYINGS

Pascal's style

350. All the good maxims already exist in the world; we just fail to apply them. (540-380)

351. The last thing we discover in composing a work is what to put down first. (976-19)

352. Authors who always refer to their works as "my book, my commentary, my history," sound like solid citizens with their own property who are always talking about "my house." They would be better to say: "our book, our commentary, our history," seeing that there is usually more of other people's property in it than their own. (Sayings, 1)

353. People ask why I use an amusing, ironic, and pleasing style. I reply that if I had written in a dogmatic way, only scholars would have read it and they don't need to, because they know as much about it as I do. Instead, I thought I must write in order to attract women and worldly people to read my letters, so that they might realize the danger of all these maxims and propositions, which are so fashionable and easily swallowed by people. (Sayings, 3.3)

People ask if I have read all the books that I quote. My

reply is no, for it would certainly have meant spending my life reading often very bad books. I got my friends to read them, but I did not use a single passage without reading it myself in the original book, going into the context, and reading the passage before and after it, to avoid all risk of quoting out of context, which is unfair and wrong. (Sayings, 3.4)

Living in a Topsy-Turvy World

354. The most unreasonable things in the world become the most reasonable, because men are so unbalanced. (977-320)

355. Christian piety destroys the human ego, whereas human politeness conceals and suppresses it. (Sayings, 7)

356. From the world's point of view, the conditions easiest to live in are the hardest from God's perspective; and vice versa. Nothing is so hard from the world's point of view than the life of faith, whereas nothing is easier from God's perspective. (693-906)

357. The world must truly be blind if it believes you. (676-397)

358. It is absurd to think there are people in the world who have rejected all the laws of God and nature only to have to invent laws for themselves which they scrupulously obey. It would seem that their license should be boundless and without restraint, considering the number of just and common sense ones they have broken. (794-393)

359. Power rules the world, not opinion. But it is opinion that exploits power. (554-303)

360. We no longer have true justice. If we had we should not accept it as a rule of justice that one should merely follow the customs of one's country. That is why we have found might when we could not find right. (86-297)

361. The imagination magnifies small things with fantastic exaggeration until they fill our whole soul. Then with bold insolence it cuts down great things to its own size, as when speaking of God. (551-84)

362. Christian character is "humbling your heart" (Romans 12:16). Human character is the opposite. (897-533)

363. I cannot forgive Descartes. In his whole philosophy he would like to do without God. But he cannot help allowing him with a flick of the fingers to set the world in motion. After that he has no more use for God. (Sayings, 2)

364. Write against those, such as Descartes, who probe science too deeply. (553-76)

365. Pious scholars are rare. (952-956)

366. Wisdom leads us back to childhood: "Unless you change and become like little children . . ." (Matthew 18:3). (82-291)

The Nature of Man

367. Man's condition is one of fickleness, boredom, and anxiety. (24-127)

368. We are equally incapable of truth and goodness. (28-436)

369. Two things teach man about his whole nature: instinct and experience. (128-396)

370. People are such inevitable fools that not to be so would amount to another form of folly. (412-414)

371. Man is debased enough to bow down to beasts and even to worship them. (53-429)

372. As man has lost his true nature, anything can become his nature. Likewise, since true good is lost, anything can be adopted as what he deems good. (397-426)

The Quest for Truth

373. Thought constitutes man's greatness. (759-346)

374. When we want to think about God, is there not something which distracts and tempts us to think of something else instead? All this is innate and evil in us. (395-478)

375. The quickest way to prevent heresy is to teach all truths, and the most certain way of refuting it is to expose them all. (733b-862b)

376. We are usually more readily convinced by reasons we have discovered for ourselves than by those which have occurred to other people. (737-10)

377. It is by the heart that God is perceived and not by reason. So that is what faith is: God perceived by the heart, not by the reason. (424-278)

378. The heart has its reasons which reason knows not of; we know this in innumerable ways. (423-277)

379. Because of man's corrupt nature, man does not act according to the reason that constitutes his being. (491-439)

380. And if we are convinced that we must never take chances, then we ought not to do anything for religion, for it is never fully certain. (577a-234a)

381. There are two sources of error: to take everything literally, and to take everything spiritually. (252-668)

382. It is false piety to preserve peace at the expense of truth. It is also false zeal to preserve truth at the expense of charity. (949-930)

383. We make an idol of truth itself, for truth apart from charity is not God but his image. It is an idol we must not love or worship for its own sake. Still less must we worship its opposite, which is falsehood. (926-582)

384. Anyone who wants to give meaning to Scripture that is not in Scripture is the enemy of Scripture. (251-900)

385. You abuse the trust people have in the church when you make them believe anything. (186-947)

386. Let us endeavor to think well; that is the basic principle of morality. (200b-347b)

The Christian Life

387. See Jesus Christ in every person, and in ourselves . . . so that he could be in every person and a model for every condition of mankind. (946-785)

388. Our prayers and virtues are abominations before God if they are not the prayers and virtues of Jesus Christ. (948-668)

389. Prayer is not in our power . . . lest those who having persevered for some time in prayer through the effective power of God, then cease to pray, lack this effective power. (969-514)

390. We may think prayer derives from ourselves. This is absurd, for even the faithful may not be virtuous, so how can we have faith by ourselves? Is it not further to move from a lack of faith to having it, than to go from faith to virtue? (930-513)

391. In order to maintain his sovereignty, God bestows the gift of prayer on whom he pleases. (930a-513a)

392. The righteous man acts by faith in the smallest details. When he reproves his servants, he desires for their conversion

to be made possible by the Spirit of God. He prays to God to correct them, hoping as much from God as from his own reproofs, and praying to God to bless his corrections. And so he acts in all other ways. (947-504)

393. It is a fine condition for the church to be in when it has no support but God. (845-861)

394. There's a mighty difference between not being for Christ and saying so, and not being for Christ and pretending to be. The former can perform miracles, but not the latter. For in the former situation it is obvious that they are against the truth and so their miracles are more obvious. (843-836)

395. There is no need of miracles to demonstrate that we must love one God alone. That is obvious! (844-837)

396. We must combine what is outward with what is inward to obtain anything from God. In other words, we must get on our knees and pray with our lips so that the proud man who will not submit to God must now submit to his creature [the priest]. If we expect help from this outward expression only, we are superstitious. If we refuse to combine it with the inward, we are being arrogant. (944-250)

397. Noble deeds are most admirable when they are kept secret. For the finest thing about them is the attempt to keep them secret. (643-159)

398. Whether I am alone or in the sight of others, in all my actions I am in the sight of God who must judge them and to whom I have devoted all of them. (931-550)

399. Aversion for the truth exists in differing degrees, but it may be said to exist in every one of us to some degree, for it is inseparable from self-love. (978-100)

LETTERS
WRITTEN TO A PROVINCIAL
BY ONE OF HIS FRIENDS

On 23 November 1654, Pascal was converted while reading John 17 alone in his bedroom. The next month he placed himself under the spiritual direction of M. Siglin, and by the next month he was taking the first of several retreats at the abbey of Port-Royal-des-Champs. Through his contacts at Port-Royal, Pascal was drawn into a controversy that was to become a national sensation.

Antoine Arnauld, an eminent lawyer and acknowledged leader of the abbey's supporters, had published two open letters defending the orthodoxy of Cornelius Jansen's book on Augustine. The book had been condemned as heretical in 1653. Arnauld had been answered by the King's confessor, the Jesuit Father Annat, and the case had been taken to the Faculty of Theology at the Sorbonne for decision. After much discussion, the Sorbonne faculty censured Arnauld on 14 January 1656. Knowing of Pascal's skill in debate, Arnauld asked the young man for help. "You are young, you have a fine mind, you ought to do something." Using several pseudonyms, Pascal replied secretly in eighteen letters, from which the following excerpts have been taken.

LETTER I
REMARKS ON A DISPUTE AMONG THEOLOGIANS AT THE SORBONNE, TO CENSURE A. ARNAULD

Paris, 23 January 1656

Sir,

We have been greatly mistaken. It was only yesterday that I was undeceived. For, until then, I had imagined that the disputes of the Sorbonne were truly of greatest importance to the interests of the Christian faith. The frequent meetings of a society so celebrated as the Faculty of Theology at Paris, in which so many extraordinary and wonderful things have happened, have so generally raised high expectation that everyone believes some significant subject is being considered. Instead, you will be astonished to learn from this communication about the issue of this affair, with which I have made myself thoroughly acquainted.

I will state it briefly as follows. Two subjects are under consideration. One is a question of *fact*. The other is a question of *right*.

The question of fact is whether Mr. Arnauld is guilty of rashness for saying in his second letter that he has carefully read the book of Jansen and has not been able to find those propositions there condemned by the late Pope [Innocent X]. Yet, as he condemns these propositions wherever they occur, he also condemns them in Jansen *if they should be there*. So the question is whether it is not extremely rash to raise a doubt respecting these propositions actually occurring in Jansen, when the Bishops have affirmed that they do?

When this matter was brought to the Sorbonne, seventy-one doctors stood in defense of Mr. Arnauld, maintaining that he could give no other reply to the numerous inquiries in his opinion of the existence of these propositions in the said book than what he did. Namely, that he had not seen them there, yet he was condemned on the assumption that they probably were.

Some went further and declared that after an exhaustive search they had not been able to discover them there, but instead he had spoken against them. They then proceeded with some warmth to require that if any doctor had seen them, he should be good enough to point them out. This seemed an obvious way of convincing everyone, even Mr. Arnauld himself. Yet this approach has never been conceded.

Instead, the proceedings against him were made by eighty secular doctors and about forty mendicant fryers who condemned Mr. Arnauld's statement without any attempt to examine whether it was true or false. They even affirmed that the question was not about the truth of his assertion but merely his rashness in putting it forward at all.

Another fifteen were reluctant to concur in the censure. We call them *the indifferent*.

This is where the question of fact finishes, about which I must confess I feel little concern. For whether Mr. Arnauld is or is not guilty of rashness does not at all affect my own conscience. And if I have any curiosity to find out whether the propositions do occur in Jansen, his book is neither so scarce nor is it so voluminous as to keep me from reading it for my own satisfaction without consulting the whole of the Sorbonne.

If I had been afraid of being considered rash myself, I would probably have been willing to agree with almost everybody I met who believed these propositions were in Jansen. But instead, I found a strange refusal on the part of everyone to show me where they were. I haven't met a single person who could say he had actually seen them for himself.

So this censure will, I'm afraid, do more harm than good and give those who may be acquainted with the facts quite a different impression from what is intended. Indeed, people are now becoming so distrustful, they will believe nothing but what they see. The point, however, is of such little importance that it doesn't touch upon our faith.

The question of *right* seems at first much more important. So I have therefore taken the utmost trouble to inform myself upon the subject. You will be glad to know this is as insignificant as the former.

The investigation questioned Mr. Arnauld's words in the same letter, "that the grace without which we can do nothing was deficient in the apostle Peter when he fell." We might have expected that the great principles of grace would have been examined, as to whether grace is bestowed on all men, and whether it is certainly efficacious. But alas! How we were deceived! For myself, I soon became a great divine, of which you will have some evidence.

To find out the truth, I went to my near neighbor Mr. N., a doctor of the College of Navarre, who is, as you know, one of the bitterest opponents of the Jansenists. As my curiosity made me almost as zealous as he was himself, I asked if, to remove all further doubts, they could come to a formal decision "that grace is given to all men."

But he replied with great rudeness, saying that was not the point, although some of his party argued that "grace is not given to all," and that even the examiners had declared in full assembly that this opinion was *problematical*. This was his own conviction, which he confirmed by a famous passage of Augustine: "We know that grace is not given to all men."

I apologized for mistaking his meaning, and asked to know whether they would at least condemn that other opinion of the Jansenists, which had created such heated debate, namely "that grace is efficacious and determines the will in the choice of good."

Again I was unfortunate: "You know nothing about it," he retorted. "That is no heresy; it is perfectly orthodox. All Thomists maintain it and I have done the same myself in my debates in the Sorbonne."

I dared not proceed; still, I could not discover where the difficulty lay. So in order to gain some insight, I begged him to state exactly in what consisted the heresy of Mr. Arnauld's proposition.

"It is this," he said, "that he does not admit that the righteous possess the power of fulfilling the commands of God, in the manner in which *we understand it*."

After this information I withdrew, elated to have found out the difficult point of the question. I hastened to Mr. N., who was sufficiently restored in health to accompany me to his brother-in-law, a most thorough Jansenist, but *in spite of that a very good man!* In order to receive a better reception, I pretended to belong to his party and asked if it was possible that the Sorbonne should introduce such an error as this into the church, "that the just always possess the power to fulfill the commands of God"?

"What are you saying?" he replied. "Do you call such a Christian sentiment as that an error, a doctrine which none but Lutherans and Calvinists would ever oppose?"

"And is not this your opinion then?" I replied.

"Certainly not, we condemn it as heretical and impious."

Quite astonished, I saw that I had now over-reacted to the Jansenist, as before I had done with the Molinist. But not being fully satisfied with his reply, I urged him to tell me ingenuously if he really maintained "that the just always had a real power to keep the divine precepts."

He grew angry at this, but with a holy zeal of course, and said he would never disguise his opinions for any consideration in the world. This was his firm belief that both he and all his party would defend to the last, as the genuine doctrine of both Thomas Aquinas and Augustine, their master.

He was so serious that I could not disbelieve him. So I returned at once to my first doctor to assure him with the utmost satisfaction that I was sure peace would soon be restored in the Sorbonne. For the Jansenists were agreed upon the just possessing power to perform the commandments. I would answer for it and would make them all sign it with their blood.

"Hold," he said, "a man must be an excellent theologian to discriminate these niceties; so fine and subtle is the difference between us that we can scarcely discern it ourselves. So you cannot be supposed to understand it, but simply are satisfied the Jansenists will tell you that the just always possess the power of fulfilling the divine commandments. This we do not dispute, but they will not inform you that this is *near power*. This is the point."

This term was to me quite new and nonsensical. I thought I had grasped the whole situation but now it was all, once more, obscure. When I asked for some explanation he made a great mystery of it and dismissed me without any further satisfaction to inquire of the Jansenists whether they admitted this *near power*.

In case I should forget about it, I ran off to my Jansenist, and after the first compliments, I asked, "Pray, do you admit the *near power?*"

He began laughing and coldly replied, "You tell me what you mean by this, and then I will be prepared to tell you what I believe."

But as I had no idea, I couldn't reply. Vaguely I shot out, "I understand it in the sense of the Molinists."

"Oh, and to which of the Molinists would you refer me?"

"All of them," I said, "as they comprise one body and have the same spirit."

"You know very little of the subject," he said. "They are so disunited among themselves that the only thing they're all agreed to is to ruin Mr. Arnauld. So they are determined mutually to use the term *near*, although they understand it themselves in many different ways, in order to seek to undermine and ruin him."

This answer amazed me. Still, I was unwilling to receive an impression of the base motives of the Molinists upon the word of one individual, and so my only concern became to find out in what different ways they employed the term *near power*.

He was quite willing to explain it to me, but remarked, "You will see such gross inconsistency and contradiction that this will amaze you and make you suspicious of my own truthfulness. But it is best to get it directly from them themselves. So if you will allow me to direct you, I would recommend a separate visit to a M. le Moine and Father Nicolai."

"I do not know either of these gentlemen," I replied.

"But possibly you may know some others I may name, who hold the same opinions." This was, in fact, the case. "Do you not know," he added, "some of the Dominicans, who are called the new Thomists, and all agree with Father Nicolai?"

I was acquainted with some of them, and being determined to seek his advice and pursue my object, I left him immediately and went to one of the disciples of M. le Moine. I urged him to tell me what it was to have the *near power* to do anything.

"Oh," he replied, "this is quite obvious: It is to have whatever power is necessary to accomplish it, in such a way that nothing is lacking to complete the action."

"So then," I answered, "to have the *near power* to cross a river is to have a boat, ferrymen, oars, and other requirements, so that nothing is lacking."

"Quite right."

"And to have the *near power* to see is to have good eyes and a good light. From your perspective, if someone possesses good eyes in the dark, he would not have the *near power* to see, because light would be needed, without which it is impossible to see at all."

"Very logical indeed."

"Consequently," I continued, "when you say that all the just at all times possess the *near power* of observing the commandments, you mean they always have the grace necessary for their performance; at least that nothing is wanting on the part of God."

"Wait a minute," he said, "the just always possess what is requisite for their obedience, or at least what is requisite to ask of God."

I replied, "I understand very well that they all have what is necessary to seek divine assistance by prayer, but need no other grace to enable them to pray."

"Perfectly correct."

"But is not an efficacious grace required to excite us to pray?"

"No," he replied, following the opinion of M. le Moine.

To lose no time, I hastened to the Jacobins, asking for those I knew to be Thomists of the new school. I asked them to give me information regarding this *near power*. First I asked if that was not something deficient in point of actual need. The answer was categorically "No." So I asked, "Why, Fathers, do you then call it *near power*, when any such deficiency occurs? Will you affirm, for example, that someone in the night without any kind of light has the *near power* to see?"

"Certainly, if he is not blind."

"I don't object to this," I said, "but M. le Moine has a quite different view of the subject."

"True, but I tell you how *we* understand it."

To this I bowed, "For I will never," I retorted, "dispute about the term if I am only informed of the meaning given to it. But I see that when you state that the just always have the *near power* to pray to God, you mean by it that they need some other aid, without which they could never pray at all."

"Excellent, excellent," replied one of the Fathers, embracing me, "most excellent, for the just need an efficacious grace not bestowed upon all men and which influences their will to pray, and whoever denies the necessity of this efficacious grace is a heretic."

"Excellent, indeed very excellent," I exclaimed in my turn. "But, according to your opinion, the Jansenists are orthodox and M. le Moine is a heretic. For they affirm that the just have power to pray, but efficacious grace is nevertheless essential, which you approve. He says the just can pray without efficacious grace, which is a statement you condemn."

"True," they said, "but then M. le Moine calls that power by the distinguishing epithet of *near power*."

"Really, good Father," I continued, "it's a mere play upon words to say that you agree respecting the same common term, but use it in a contrary sense."

So I had nothing more to say. But fortunately in came the disciple of M. le Moine whom I had previously consulted. This struck me at the time as an amazing coincidence. But I have since learned that these fortunate accidents are not uncommon, as they are in the habit of continual intercourse.

I spoke immediately to M. le Moine's disciple: "I know a gentleman who maintains that all the just have always at all times the power to pray. Yet they never will pray without an efficacious grace to impel them, which God does not always grant to all the just. Is this heretical?"

"Stop," said the doctor, "you take me by surprise! Wait a minute, wait a minute—if he calls that power *near power* he is a Thomist, and is therefore orthodox. If not, he is a Jansenist, and consequently a heretic."

"But he neither calls it near, nor not near."

"Then he is a heretic—I appeal to these good Fathers."

I did not, however, take the opinion of these judges, for they had already given consent by a significant nod, and then proceeded, "The gentleman refuses to adopt the term *near* because he can obtain no explanation of it."

One of the Fathers at this point was going to favor us with a definition, but the disciple of M. le Moine interrupted him, saying, "Why do you wish to renew our quarrelsome arguments? Have we not agreed not to explain the term *near*, and to use it on both sides without defining what it signifies?" He immediately concurred.

Now I was let into the secret. Rising to take my leave, I exclaimed, "Fathers, I feel extremely apprehensive that this whole affair is mere chicanery, and whatever may come from your meetings I will venture to predict that whatever censure may be inflicted, peace will not be established. For if it is agreed to pronounce the syllable *near* without giving any definition of the term, each party will claim the victory. The Dominicans will say it is understood in their sense, M. le Moine will affirm it in his, and there will arise more debates concerning the significance of the word than about it being introduced at all. But it will be unworthy of the Sorbonne and the Faculty of Theology to make use of ambiguous terms without giving some explanation. I ask you once and for all what is it I must believe in order to be an orthodox Christian?"

All speaking together, they said, "You must say that all the just possess the *near power* without attaching any meaning to the words."

Taking my leave I replied, "That is to say, this word must be pronounced with the lips in fear of being stigmatized with the name of heretic. Is it a scriptural term?"

"No."

"Is it used by the Fathers, the Councils, or the Popes?"

"No."

"Is it used by Thomas Aquinas?"

"No."

"Where then arises the necessity of using it at all, since it is neither supported by any authority, nor has any distinctive meaning of its own?"

"You are just plain obstinate," they exclaimed, "but you shall pronounce it or be accounted a heretic, and Mr. Arnauld also. For our party comprises the majority, and if it is necessary we can compel as many of the others to vote as will carry the point."

This last reason was so forcible that I bowed and withdrew to give you this account, by which you will see that none of the following points have been examined and consequently neither condemned nor approved:

1. That grace is not given to all men;
2. That all the just have power to keep the divine commandments;
3. That nevertheless they need efficacious grace to determine their will to obey them, and even to pray;
4. That this efficacious grace is not always given to all the just, and that it depends solely on the mercy of God.

So there is nothing but the poor word *near*, without any meaning, that runs any risk.

Fortunate are those who live entirely ignorant of it! Fortunate are those who existed before the birth of this word *near*! So I see no solution if the gentlemen of the academy do not by some authoritative mandate banish this stupid term out of the Sorbonne, a term which has caused so many divisions. Unless this is done, the censure must be confirmed. But I can see no other consequence than that of making the Sorbonne contemptible, which will destroy the authority it has had on other occasions.

I now leave you at liberty to vote for or against the term *near*, for I have too much affection for you to persecute you upon so frivolous a pretext.

If this description should give you any amusement, I shall continue to give you every information of what goes on.

I am, et cetera.

LETTER II
ON THE SUBJECT OF SUFFICIENT GRACE

Paris, 29 January 1656

Sir,

At the very moment I was sealing up my last letter, our old friend Mr. N. came in. This was most fortunate for my curiosity for he is thoroughly acquainted with the controversies of the day and is perfectly in the secret of the Jesuits. For he is with them constantly and intimate with their chief men. After mentioning the particular purpose of his visit, I asked him to state in a few words the points in debate between the two parties.

With utmost readiness he told me that these were chiefly two: The one respecting *near power*; the other *sufficient grace*. The first I have already explained; so allow me to speak about the second.

The difference on the subject of sufficient grace is chiefly this. The Jesuits maintain there is a general grace bestowed upon all mankind, but in a sense subordinated to free will, so that this grace is rendered effective or ineffective as the world chooses, without any additional assistance from God. It does not need anything external to itself to make its operations effectual. On this account it is distinguished by the word *sufficient*. In contrast, the Jansenists affirm that no grace is actually sufficient unless it is also effective. That is, all those principles that do not determine the will to act effectively are insufficient for action because, they say, no one can act without efficacious grace.

Afterwards, as I wished to be informed on the doctrine of the new Thomists, I asked him about them.

"It is quite ridiculous," he exclaimed, "for they agree with the Jansenist to admit of a sufficient grace given to all men, but they insist that they can never act with this alone. For it is still necessary that God should bestow an efficacious grace to influence the will, and this is not bestowed upon all."

Then I said, "This grace is at once sufficient and insufficient."

"Very true," he answered. "For if it is sufficient, nothing more is required to produce the action, and if it isn't, it cannot be called sufficient."

"What then is the difference between them and the Jansenists?"

He replied, "They differ in this, that the Dominicans at least acknowledge that all men have sufficient grace."

"I understand you; but you say so without thinking so, because they proceed immediately to state that in order to act we must possess efficacious grace, which is not given to all. So, although they agree with the Jesuits in using the same nonsensical terms, they contradict them in the substantial meaning, and agree with the Jansenist."

"True."

So I asked, "How is it that the Jesuits and these men are so united, and why do they not oppose them as well as the Jansenists, for they will always find them powerful opponents. While asserting the necessity of efficacious grace to determine the will, they prevent the establishment of what they deem to be of itself sufficient."

He replied, "The Dominicans are a powerful body, and the Jesuits are too cunning to openly encounter them. They are content to bring them to admit the term *sufficient grace*, although the sense in which they use it is widely different. By this means they gain the advantage of easily making their opponent's sentiments appear indefensible whenever they please. Suppose that all men have sufficient principles of grace; it is quite natural to infer that efficacious grace is not necessary to action, because the sufficiency of the general principle will preclude the necessity of anything additional. He who uses the term *sufficient* includes whatever is essentially requisite, and it will be of no avail for the Dominicans to protest that they impute a different sense to the expression. People accustomed to the general use of the word will not listen to their explanation. Thus the society of Jesuits have profited greatly by the expression adopted by the Dominicans, without urging them further. And if you were acquainted with what occurred during the Popes Clement VIII and Paul V, and how the Dominicans opposed the efforts of the Jesuits to establish the doctrine of sufficient grace, you would not be surprised at the present cessation of hostilities, nor the ready consent of the latter to their enjoying their own opinion provided they have equal liberty, especially as the Dominicans have adopted and agreed publicly to their favorite term."

Asking for one of the new Thomists, who was delighted to see me, I asked the following. "My good Father, it is not enough for all men to have a *near power*, by which they can in fact do nothing, they must possess *sufficient grace*, by which they can do—as little. Is not this the doctrine of your schools?"

"Certainly it is," he replied, "and I firmly maintained it in the Sorbonne this very morning."

I asked in turn, "Is this grace, which is given to all men, sufficient?"

"Yes," he said.

"And yet it is of no avail without efficacious grace?"

"No."

"And all men have *sufficient*, but not all have *efficacious* grace?"

"Exactly so."

"That is to say, all men have grace enough, and all have not grace enough—this grace is sufficient and it is insufficient; that is, it is nominally sufficient and really insufficient. Upon my word, Father, this is a fine doctrine! Have you forgotten since you quitted the world what the word *sufficient* means? Do you remember that it includes all that is necessary to an action? Surely you haven't forgotten this! To take an obvious illustration: If your table was only supplied with two ounces of bread and a glass of water each day, would you be satisfied with your Prior if he asked what one thing more you would require to make your meal sufficient—which, however, he would not furnish? How then can you state that all men have sufficient grace for acting, while you at the same time confess that something more—which all do not possess—is absolutely necessary? Is this so unimportant an article of faith that everyone is left at liberty to decide whether *efficacious grace* is or is not required? Or is it entirely a matter of indifference?"

"What do you mean" replied the good Father, "by indifferent? That is heresy, rank heresy. To admit the necessity of efficacious grace to act effectually is faith; but to deny it is downright heresy."

"Where are we now," I exclaimed, "and which side am I to take here? If I deny sufficient grace, I am a Jansenist. If I admit it with the Jesuits in such a sense that there is no necessity for efficacious grace, I am, you tell me, a heretic. If I agree with you, I fly against common sense. I am a madman, say the Jesuits. What then am I to do in this inevitable situation of being either considered a madman, a heretic, or a Jansenist? And to what situation are we reduced if the Jansenists alone avoid confounding faith and reason, and thus save themselves at once from absurdity and error?"

My good friend the Jansenist seemed pleased with my remarks, and thought that he had already won me to his cause. However, he said nothing to me, but turning to the Father: "Pray," he said, "in what respect do you agree with the Jesuits?"

He replied, "In this, that we both acknowledge that *sufficient grace* is given to all men."

"But," he replied, "there are two things in the term *sufficient grace*: The sound which is mere air, and the sense which is real and significant. So that when you avow an agreement with the Jesuits in the use of the word, but oppose them in its sense, it is obvious that you disagree with them in the essential matter, though you accord in the use of the term. Is this really acting with openness and sincerity?"

"But," said the good man, "what cause of complaint have you, since we deceive no one by this way of speaking? For in our schools we publicly declare that we understand the expression in a sense quite opposite to the Jesuits."

"I complained," said my friend, "that you do not declare to all the world that by *sufficient grace* you mean a grace which is not sufficient. Having changed the significance of the usual terms in religion, you are forced in conscience to declare that when you admit of sufficient grace in all men, you really intend that they have not sufficient grace; and no one is aware of your own peculiar interpretation. Everywhere it is said that they maintain the doctrine of sufficient grace.

"Shall I describe for you the situation of the church in the midst of these different views? I think of it like a man who, leaving his native country to travel abroad, encounters robbers who wound him so severely that they leave him half dead. He sends for three doctors who are resident in the neighborhood. The first, after probing his wounds, pronounces them to be mortal and tells him that only God can restore him. The second, wishing to flatter him, assures him that he has sufficient strength to reach home and insults the first for opposing his opinion and threatens to ruin him. When the unfortunate patient sees the third physician approach, he stretches out his hands to welcome him as the one who will decide the dispute.

"This physician, upon looking at his wounds and learning of the opinions already given, agrees with the second and together they turn upon the first with contempt. They now form the strongest party. The patient infers from this that the third physician agrees with the second, and on asking him the question, assures him most positively that he has enough strength for the proposed journey. But the wounded man, expatiating upon his weakness, asks how he came to this conclusion.

"'Why, you still have legs, and legs are the means which, according to the nature of things, are sufficient for the purpose of walking.'

"The wounded traveler replies, 'That may be, but have I all the strength required for using them? They really seem useless to me in my present weakened condition.'

"'Certainly they are,' replies the physician, 'and you will never be able to walk unless God gives you some extraordinary assistance to sustain and guide you.'

"'What then,' says the sick man, 'have I not sufficient strength in myself to be able to walk?'

"'Oh no, far from it.'

"'Then you have a different opinion from your friend respecting my real condition.'

"'I must admit, I have.'

"What do you suppose the wounded man would say to all this? He would certainly complain of the strange procedure and of the ambiguous language of the third physician. He scolds him for agreeing with the second, when in fact he is of a contrary opinion, although they appear to agree and drive away the first in doing so. When he tries his strength and finds that he is only weak, he gets rid of them both. He then recalls the first one, who puts him under his care, follows his advice, and asks God for strength which he knows he needs. His petitions are heard, and eventually he reaches home in peace."

The good Father was astonished at this parable and made no reply. So, anxious to encourage him, I said in the gentlest manner, "But after all, what do you think, my good Father, of applying the term *sufficient* to a grace that you say is a point of faith but which is really *insufficient?*"

"You are at liberty to speak whatever you wish to say on such matters, since you are a private individual. But I am a monk and I belong to a society. Don't you see a great difference? We are dependent upon our superiors, and they depend elsewhere and have promised our votes. What do you suppose would happen to me?" For he remembered that half a word was sufficient to banish one of his brethren to Abbeville on a similar occasion.

But I inquired, "How is it that your community pledges itself at all upon the subject of this grace?"

"Oh, that's another matter. All I can say is that our order has most strenuously maintained the doctrine of Thomas Aquinas respecting efficacious grace. How zealously it opposed that of Molina at the very moment of its introduction! How it has labored to established the necessity of the efficacious grace of Jesus Christ! But the Jesuits, who from the very commencement of the heresies of Luther and Calvin took advantage of the people's incapacity to discern between the truth and falsity of the doctrine of Thomas Aquinas, circulated their sentiments with such rapidity that they soon attained a dominion over the popular faith. So we should now have been decried as Calvinists and treated as the Jansenists now are, if we had not qualified the truth of an efficacious grace by the acknowledgment at least in appearance of a sufficient one. In this dilemma what better expedient could be devised, at once to preserve the truth and save our credit, than that of admitting the name of sufficient grace but denying the reality. This then is the state of the case."

He spoke in such a sad tone that I really pitied him; but not so my friend who continued, "Do not flatter yourself with having preserved the truth: If she had no other protectors, she would have perished in such feeble hands. You have received the name of her enemy into the church, which is as baneful as having received the enemy himself. Names are inseparable from things. If the term *sufficient grace* be once established, it is in vain to say that you understand a grace which is insufficient. It will never do. The explanation will be detested. The world uses more sincerity on the most unimportant occasions. The Jesuits will triumph. For this will establish their *sufficient grace*, while yours will only be nominal, and thus you will propagate an article of faith which is contrary to your own belief."

"No," said the Father, "we would all suffer martyrdom rather than consent to the establishment of *sufficient grace* in the sense of the term used by the Jesuits. Thomas Aquinas, whom we have sworn to follow even to death, is diametrically opposed to it."

My friend, more grave than I could be, replied: "Your fraternity, Father, has received an Order which is miserably managed. It abandons the grace which was entrusted to it, and which was never before abandoned from the creation of the world. For that victorious grace which the patriarchs anticipated, which the prophets predicted, which was introduced by Jesus Christ, preached by the apostle Paul, explained by Augustine, the greatest of the Fathers, embraced by all his followers, confirmed by Bernard of Clairvaux, the last of the Fathers, maintained by Thomas Aquinas, the angel of the schools, and then transmitted from him to your society, maintained by so many of your fathers, and so gloriously defended by your fraternity under the Popes Clement and Paul. This *efficacious grace* which has been thus committed to you as a sacred trust, in order to secure by means of an indissoluble holy order and succession of preachers, to proclaim it to the end of the world, is at last deserted for the most unworthy reasons. It is high time for others to arm in its defense. It is time for God to raise up some intrepid supporters of the doctrine of grace who, fortunately unacquainted with the pragmatism of this age, shall serve God from motives of genuine love. The Dominicans may no longer be able to defend it, but it is not without protectors, for it will raise and qualify others by its own almighty power.

"Grace demands holy and sanctified hearts—hearts which she purifies herself and detaches from those worldly interests so incompatible with the gospel. Reflect seriously, my Father, and take care lest God remove the candlestick from its place and leave you in darkness and dishonor as a punishment for your indifference to a cause of such vital importance to his church."

He would have said much more, for he kindled as he proceeded, but I thought proper to interrupt him and getting up said, "Truly, Father, had I any influence in France, I would have it proclaimed with a sound of a trumpet: 'KNOW ALL MEN, that when the Jacobins state that *sufficient grace* is given to all, they mean that all have not the grace which is really sufficient.' After which you might state the same but not otherwise, as often as you pleased."

So our visit came to an end.

You will see from this communication that there is a political sufficiency not unlike a *near power*. Yet it seems to me that anyone who is not a Jacobin may, without incurring any risk, doubt of both *near power* and *sufficient grace*.

As I am folding up my letter, I hear that the censure is inflicted. But as I know nothing respecting the wording of it, and as it will not be made public until the 15th of February, I shall write no more until the next post.

I am, et cetera.

LETTER IV
CONCERNING ACTUAL GRACE
AND SINS OF IGNORANCE

Paris, 25 February 1656

Sir,

The Jesuits are an incomparable people. I have seen Jacobins, doctors, and all manner of other kinds of people, yet my knowledge was still incomplete. For others are merely copyists of them. At the springhead the stream is purest. So I went to one of their most intelligent followers, accompanied by my faithful Jansenist friend who had been with me on my previous visits.

Anxious to obtain full information in regard to the controversy between them and the Jansenists on the subject of what they call *actual grace*, I asked the good Father if he would instruct me. Since I did not even know the significance of this term, I asked him to explain it.

"Of course," he said. "For I am pleased with people that are searching. Our definition is as follows: Actual grace is inspired by God, by which he teaches us his will and by which he stimulates within us a desire to fulfill it."

"What then is the precise point of the argument," I asked, "between you and the Jansenists?"

He answered, "It is this. We maintain that God bestows actual grace upon all in every temptation. Otherwise, if they did not have actual grace to prevent the commission of sin, guilt could never be imputed to them. But the Jansenists affirm that sins committed without actual grace must be imputed. Surely they are dreaming!"

I saw the drift of his argument, but in order to see it more clearly I replied, "My dear Father, this phrase *actual grace* perplexes me, for I am quite unused to it. So if you will have the goodness to explain its meaning, without using the term, I would be most grateful."

"Oh, if that's what you want, very well, for the sense will remain the same. We insist then, as an incontrovertible principle, that no action can be considered sinful if prior to its commission, God does not communicate the knowledge of what is evil in it and so does not inspire us to avoid it. Do you understand me now?"

Astonished at this doctrine, which implied that all unpremeditated sins and those committed from forgetfulness of God are not chargeable upon the criminal, I turned to my friend the Jansenist. I saw from his manner that he did not believe this statement. But he was silent, and so I asked the Father to give me some more concrete evidence of his argument.

"Do you need proofs?" he asked. "Certainly I will furnish them, irrefutable proofs; trust me."

Saying this, he withdrew to search for some books, and I took the opportunity to ask my friend what he thought of his opinion.

He replied, "If you see that this is such a novelty to you, then be sure that neither the Fathers, the Popes, the Councils, the Scriptures, or indeed any book of devotion, ancient or modern, has given this argument either. The only ones that do so are the Casuists and the new scholars, from whom he will produce a vast amount of evidence."

"Oh, but I despise such writers as these if they contradict tradition."

"You are quite right," he said. At that moment the good Father returned laden with his books.

"There, read that"—offering me the first of the batch. "It's a summary of sins by Father Bauny, and as proof of its excellence, this is the fifth edition."

In a whisper my Jansenist friend said, "This book has been condemned at Rome and by the Bishops of France."

"Turn to page 906," said the Father.

I did so and found these words: "To sin so as to be accounted guilty before God, it is necessary to know that what is going to be committed is not good, or at least to be doubtful about it, or to suppose that God will be displeased with the premeditated action, and so forbids it. So if it is then done in defiance of every opposition, then it is sin."

I retorted, "This is a fine beginning!"

"See," he said, "the power of envy. This is what made Mr. Hallier, before he sided with us, ridicule Father Bauny by saying about him: 'See the man who takes away the sins of the world!' "

"Indeed," I replied, "this redemption of Mr. Bauny is a novel description indeed!"

He asked if I wanted a greater authority. "Then read this by Father Annat, the last of which he produced against Mr. Arnauld. Look at the page which I have turned down, marked with a pencil; every syllable is gold."

The words were as follows: "He who has no thought of God, or of his sins, or any conception of it or knowledge of his duty to exercise acts of contrition or love to God, possesses no actual grace to exercise such acts. However, it is true that he does not sin in omitting them, but if he is finally condemned, it will not be as a punishment for this omission." A few lines lower down it adds, "The same may be affirmed of committing sin."

"Do you see the way in which the author speaks regarding sins of omission and of commission? He leaves nothing out. What do you say?"

"O, it is so charming, for the results are expected, how logical! I can already discern surprising mysteries! For it means that a much greater number of people are justified by their ignorance or forgetfulness of God than by grace and the sacraments of our faith. But please, Father, is this a well-founded argument? Is there not some resemblance here to that sufficiency which will not suffice? I am apprehensive of the nice distinction which already is a trap. Do you really mean this?"

"Indeed," replied the Father, with some warmth, "this is no jest. Mockery, sir, must not be made about this subject."

"Indeed, I'm not joking, but I do fear that what seems attractive may not prove to be true."

"Well then, if you want further proof, look at the writings of M. le Moine, who has taught this before the full Council. In fact, he learned it from us, but he has had the ability to sort out its intricacies. And how irrefutable is the evidence he has built up! He argues that for an action to be sinful, all the following thoughts must pass in the mind. But read it yourself, and examine it carefully."

So I read the original Latin, of which I now give you a translation:

1. On the one side God gives to the soul a certain love which disposes it to do what is commanded. And on the other hand, a rebellious lust is associated with those who are disobedient.
2. God inspires the soul with the knowledge of its own weaknesses.
3. God inspires it with the knowledge of the physician who must heal it.
4. Then God inspires it with the desire to be healed.
5. God inspires it next with the desire to pray and to ask for his help.

"Then," added the Jesuit, "if all these do not happen together, the action cannot properly be called sinful and cannot therefore be entreated, as M. le Moine states in the succeeding passage. Do you want to have any other authorities? For here they are."

"Yes, yes," whispered my Jansenist, "but they are all modern authorities."

"I see that," I replied. "But, my good Father, this would be a fine thing for some of my acquaintances. I really must introduce them to it! Perhaps you scarcely ever saw such

innocent people. They never think of God. Sin has blinded
their minds. They have never known anything of their moral
sicknesses nor of the Physician who can cure them. They
have not even wished to have health of soul, much less have
they asked God to give it to them. So to adopt M. le Moine's
language, they are just as innocent now as they were in their
baptism as infants. They have never entertained a single
thought about loving God or about having contrition for sin.
So according to Father Annat, they have never committed
any sin through default of charity or penitence. Their life is
one continual search after various pleasures, without any
interruption from remorse. Their dissolute lives make me
believe their destruction is inevitable. Yet my good Father,
you teach that these very excesses will make their salvation
all the more certain. What a blessing is your doctrine to
justify mankind in this way! While others are prescribing
painful austerities to save the soul, because they see the
desperate state they are in, you are saying everything is just
fine! What a wonderful way to procure happiness both in
this world and another!

"I had always supposed that our sinfulness was made worse
in proportion to our neglect of God. And now I see that
whenever someone comes to this point of total
thoughtlessness, everything becomes allowable and indeed
innocent. Away then with those who sin by halves and still
retain some attachment to virtue! These demi-transgressors
will all be lost. But on the other hand, blatant sinners,
hardened offenders, reckless sinners, whose iniquity overflows
in abundance, there is no hell for them. They have cheated
the devil by giving themselves entirely to his influence!"

The good Father, who clearly saw the connection between
his principles and my logical arguments, smartly made his
exit. Without showing any signs of conviction, either
because of his own natural meekness or perhaps from motives
of policy, he merely said: "To understand our way of avoiding
these incongruities, you have to understand that our
statement with respect to the transgressors of whom you
speak is that they would not incur guilt if they had never

thought of repentance or committing themselves to God. But we maintain that they have all cherished such thoughts and that God never commits anyone to commit sin without previously giving him a view of the sin he is about to perpetrate. For God gives them a desire to avoid it, or at least the opportunity to ask his help to avoid it. It is only the Jansenists who will contradict this statement."

I replied, "So does the heresy of the Jansenists consist in denying that every time sin is committed, the offender feels remorse of conscience, and that it is only in defiance of it that he leaps over every barrier, as Father Bauny argues? This is a curious kind of heresy indeed! I am used to suppose that a man is condemned for being devoid of all good thoughts, but to be condemned for not believing that everyone else possesses them, this I have never imagined before. So Father, I feel I must in good conscience undeceive you and insist that there are thousands who have no such desires, and who sin without any remorse. Indeed, they make a boast of their crimes. Can anyone be better aware of this than you yourselves? Isn't it surely to you that they come and confess and that this is found among people of the greatest distinction? So I do warn you, good Father, of the dangerous consequences of your doctrine. Are you unaware of the effect this will have on the licentious, who are only too eager to avail themselves of every way of discrediting religion?"

Here my friend interposed to support my remarks by saying: "Father, you would better promote your ideas by avoiding so clear a statement as you have now given of the significance of the term *actual grace*. For how can you expect people to believe so plainly 'that no one can commit sin without previously being aware of his evil and his Physician, and cherishing a desire to be healed and ask God for a cure'? Do you really think your mere statement is sufficient to convince the world that the avaricious, the impure, those who commit blasphemy, or indulge in murderous revenge, robbery, and sacrilege, really want to have chastity, humility, and the other Christian virtues? Is it credible to believe that those philosophers who were so optimistic of the power of human nature knew also its weakness and its remedy? Can you maintain that such as confidently assert this maxim—that 'God does not bestow virtue, nor did anyone ever solicit it of him'—really thought of asking it themselves? Who can imagine that the Epicureans, who denied the existence of a Divine Providence, felt any desire to pray to God? Instead, they aver that 'it is an affront to ask his interference in our necessities as if he could descend to concern himself about our affairs.' Who can imagine that idolaters and atheists, in the midst of all the incalculable diversity of their temptations to sin, entertain a single desire to seek the true God, about whom they are utterly ignorant, in order to receive real virtues, to which they are blinded?"

"Yes," said the good Father in a firm and resolute tone, "yes, we do and will say so. Rather than admit that it is possible to commit sin without clearly seeing its vileness and cherishing an opposing wish, we will maintain that the whole world, even the most impious and infidel of the human race, have these inward insights and desires in the very moment of temptation. You can show no evidence to the contrary from Scripture."

Here I interrupted and said, "What, Father, is it necessary to recur to Scripture to prove what is so obvious? This is no point of faith or of dispute. It is a matter of fact. We see it, know it, and feel it."

My Jansenist friend, adhering to the rules, replied, "If you really want to be guided solely by the Scriptures, I consent heartily. Since it is written, 'God has not revealed his judgments to the heathen but has left them to wander in their own ways,' do not then say that God has enlightened those whom the sacred writings affirm to be left in darkness and in the shadow of death. Is not your error of conviction not sufficiently exposed by the apostle Paul, when he describes himself as the chief of sinners, for a sin which he declares he committed through ignorance and unbelief? Is it not obvious from the gospel that those who crucified Jesus Christ needed that forgiveness which he prayed for them, though they knew not the wickedness of their conduct, and which, according to the apostle, they would never have perpetrated had they been aware of it? Does not Jesus Christ warn us that persecutors will arise, imagining that they do God service by seeking to destroy his church? This shows that the sin which the apostle describes as the greatest of all others may be committed by those who, so far from being conscious of its wickedness, really suppose they sinned in omitting to do it. Finally, has not Jesus Christ himself taught us that there are two descriptions of sinners: The one sins knowingly, the other ignorantly. Yet both will suffer punishment, though in differing proportions."

Urged by so much scriptural evidence to which the good Father had appealed, he began to give way. Allowing that the wicked were not under an immediate inspiration to sin, he said to us: "You will at least not deny that the righteous never sin, unless God gives them . . ."

"Oh ho," interrupting him, "you are retracting your statement; you are abandoning your general principle. Where it is unavailing with respect to sinners, you want to compromise, at least on behalf of the righteous. But even in this case, it would be so restricted in its application as scarcely to be of any help, and so it is therefore not worth an argument."

My friend, who seemed as deep in the subject as if he had been studying it that very morning, replied, "Oh, Father, this is the last refuge to which your party seeks shelter. But it is no use. The example of the righteous is by no means more advantageous to your cause. Who can doubt that they are often caught in sin? Do they not assure us that lust often spreads its secret snares in their path, and that it is common for sober-minded people to yield to pleasure when they only intended to yield to necessity, as Augustine admits with respect to himself in his *Confessions*? How often do we see keen people become frustrated in a discussion in defending their own interests, when at the time they really believed they were arguing only for the interests of truth, and hold on to the same conviction for a long time! So what shall we say about those who deliberately sin, imagining it to be really good, of which the history of the church is replete, and all of them admitted by the Fathers to be sinful? If this were not so, how could any secret iniquities be imputed to the righteous? How could it be true that only God knows their extent and number, that no one really knows whether he is deserving of love or hatred, and even the most saintly people live in perpetual fear and trembling, although they do not feel in any way guilty, as the apostle Paul says of himself?

"It is clear that the righteous transgress through ignorance, and the most eminent saints seldom sin otherwise. For how is it conceivable that such holy persons, who avoid, with so much care and diligence, the least thing they believe to be displeasing to God, nevertheless commit many sins every day? How is it possible that, having a knowledge of their weakness and of the position and desire to be healed, and seeking divine help, yet in defiance of all these pious inspirations, these zealous souls should be left to sweep aside every barrier and rush into sin?

"The inference is, Father, that neither sinners nor saints are always in possession of this knowledge, these desires and inspirations. To adopt your own phraseology, they have not *actual grace* in every occasion. So no longer believe in your new authorities, who assert it is impossible to sin while in ignorance of what is right. Say instead, in agreement with Augustine and the ancient Fathers, that it is impossible not to sin while continuing ignorant of what is right."

Although the good Father found that his views, both with regard to the righteous and the wicked, were equally untenable, he was still not wholly discouraged. After a short pause, he began. "I will now convince you," he said. Taking up Father Bauny at the very page he had recited before, "Look at the reason on which his opinion is founded. I assure you he is not defective in proof. Read his quotation from Aristotle, and after such a distinguished authority you must either agree with us or burn the writings of this prince of philosophers."

"I am very much afraid," I said, "you will disagree again."

"Oh, don't be alarmed, all is well—Aristotle is on my side. Listen to Father Bauny: 'In order that an action is voluntary, it must be the action of a man who sees, knows, and understands well what degree of good and evil attaches to it.' The voluntary, as we say in common with the philosopher (Aristotle, you know)," he said with great self-complacency, squeezing my hand, "is that which is done by someone knowing the constitutive elements of the action. Consequently, when the will chooses or rejects unreflectively and without examination, before the understanding is able to discover the evil of compliance or refusal, doing or neglecting an action, it is neither good nor bad. For prior to this examination, the action is not voluntary. Are you now satisfied?"

"Why, really", I replied, "Aristotle is of the same opinion as Father Bauny, but this does not lessen my surprise. Can Aristotle really be accused of having such a view? I thought he was a man of sense."

"I will soon explain this," said my Jansenist friend. Requesting to look into Aristotle's *Ethics*, he opened the volume at the beginning of the third book where Father Bauny had taken the very words already cited, saying, "I can forgive you, my good Father, for believing on the testimony of Father Bauny that this was the view of Aristotle. But you would have thought differently had you read him yourself. For he states indeed that 'for an action to be voluntary, it is necessary to know its peculiarities.' But nothing else is meant by this than the particular circumstances of the action, as it appears obvious from the examples he gives to justify his position.

"It is obvious that a description of ignorance of particular circumstances renders actions involuntary, which the Fathers describe as the ignorance of fact. But in regard to the ignorance of right, of good and evil in an action, which is the subject of our consideration, let's see whether Aristotle and Father Bauny really do agree.

"'All the wicked,' says the philosopher, 'are ignorant of what they ought to do and what they ought to avoid; and it is this which renders them wicked and vicious. On this account, it cannot be said that because a man is ignorant of what is proper to be done to discharge his duty, his action is therefore involuntary. For this ignorance in the choice of good and evil does not constitute an action involuntary but vicious. The same may be said of him who is ignorant of the rules of duty, as this ignorance is blameworthy and inexcusable. So the ignorance which constitutes involuntary actions and is pardonable, is only with regards to the fact in particular, with all its individual circumstances. We excuse and forgive the person whom we consider as having acted contrary to his will.'

"Will you now argue, Father, that Aristotle is of your opinion? What must be amazing to see is that a pagan philosopher was more enlightened than your doctors of divinity upon a point so crucial to morality and the conduct of souls, or the knowledge of those conditions which render actions voluntary or involuntary, and consequently which excuse or condemn them! Do you expect any support from this prince of philosophers and no longer oppose the prince of divines who decides the point in the following words: 'They who sin through ignorance commit the action with the consent of the will, although they did not have the intention of committing sin. So sin of this description cannot be perpetrated without the will, but the will induces the action only, not the sin, which did not however prevent the action being sinful, in spite of the prohibitions being a sufficient condemnation'?"

The Jesuit seemed more surprised at the quotation from Aristotle than that from Augustine. He was wondering what reply to give when a servant came in to say that so and so asked for an interview. So leaving us abruptly he said, "I will speak to some of our Fathers about this matter. They will be able to suggest a reply. We have some subtle divines amongst us who are profoundly aware of the controversy."

We understood him. So being alone with my friend, I expressed my amazement at the total corruption of morals which this doctrine tended to give.

"How," he said, "how absolutely amazed am I at your astonishment! Don't you know, then, that they are much greater delinquents in morality than even in other matters?"

Immediately he cited some glaring examples, deferring more ample illustrations to another occasion. The first time I can have such an interview, these will supply matter for further conversation.

I am, et cetera.

LETTER V
THE MOTIVE OF THE JESUITS
IN ESTABLISHING A NEW MORALITY

Paris, 20 March 1656

Sir,

In fulfillment of my promise, I enclose the first outlines of Jesuit morality, as the views of those men who are so "eminent in learning and wisdom, who are all under the guidance of the Divine wisdom, which is so much more certain than all the light of philosophy."

Perhaps you think I am joking; indeed I am serious, for this is their own language in their publication entitled *Image of the First Century*. I have copied their words, which I shall continue to do in the following eulogy: "It is a society of men, or rather of angels, of whom Isaiah prophesied, 'Go, you angels, prompt and swift.' Is not this prediction obvious? They have the spirit of eagles. . . . They have changed the face of Christianity." Their saying this about themselves is enough, as you will see by their maxims which I am going to introduce to you.

Anxious as I am to be fully informed, I am reluctant to depend entirely upon my friend's description; therefore I determined to converse with them personally. But I found everything he had said to be correct. Indeed, he had never deceived me. So you will have an account of these conversations.

My friend had made such extravagant statements that I could scarcely believe them. He pointed to their own publications as his source, and no defense could be made, so the opinion of individuals ought not to be imputed to the whole body. I assured him that I knew some who were as rigid as those whom he quoted were lax. This gave him the opportunity to exhibit the true nature of the Society, which is by no means generally known, and which perhaps to you may be an important piece of information. He began as follows:

"You suppose that it speaks considerably in their favor to show that some of their Fathers do agree with the maxims of the gospel, as well as others who contradict them. So you could infer that these lax opinions are not attributable to the whole Society. I am well aware of this, for if it were the case, they would not tolerate such contradictions. Since they have those who maintain so liberal a view, you must conclude that the whole spirit of the Society is not that of real Christianity. If it were, they would not tolerate those who so diametrically opposed it."

I asked, "What then is the objective of the whole body? Doubtless they have no fixed principles, so everyone is free to say what he pleases."

"No, this is not so. Such a large body could not exist if it were so rash as to leave itself without a soul to govern and to regulate its concerns. Besides, there is a specific order that nothing shall be printed without the approval of their superiors."

"But how can the superiors themselves permit such opposing views?"

"I will explain it," he said.

"Their object is not to corrupt morals. This is certainly not their design. But neither is it their sole purpose to reform them. This would be bad policy. So their intention is this. Having the best opinion of themselves, they think it is both profitable and necessary in the interests of the faith that their reputation should be extended throughout the world, and that they should obtain the spiritual direction of everyone's conscience. As the strict injunctions of the gospel are adapted to rule some people, they will make use of them whenever the occasion favors it. But since these sayings do not correspond with the views of the majority of mankind, they dispense with them for the sake of securing general acceptance. On this account, they are related with people in every condition of life, in every country and climate, and so it is necessary to employ casuists whose range of views should suit every existing diversity of circumstance. So you will readily see that if they had none but casuists of lax notions, they would defeat their main purpose, which is to please everybody, because the truly religious are solicitous of more rigorous leadership. But as there are not many of this kind, they do not need many guides of the stricter class to direct them. A few will suffice for the few that there are, while the crowd of lax casuists offer their services to the many who wish to be excused of discipline.

"It is by this obliging and accommodating conduct, as Father Petau calls it, that they open their arms to all the world. If someone should approach them intent upon the restoration of what he had obtained fraudulently, don't imagine that they would try to dissuade him from his purpose. On the contrary, they would applaud and confirm his determination. But if someone else should present himself asking for absolution without restitution, it would be odd indeed if they did not furnish him with expedients and guarantee his success.

"In this way they keep all their friends and protect themselves against all their enemies. If they should be reproached for their extreme laxity, immediately they show to the public their strict directors, along with the books they have composed on the strictness of the Christian law. With these evidences they will satisfy the superficial, who cannot probe their depths.

"So they accommodate to all kinds of people and are well prepared with an answer to every question, so that in countries where a crucified Jesus appears foolishness, they will suppress the scandal of the cross and preach only Jesus Christ in his glory and not in a state of suffering. So in India and

China, where they allow Christians to practice idolatry itself, they do it with the ingenious device of making them conceal an image of Christ under their cloaks, to which they are instructed to address mentally the adorations publicly rendered to their false gods. . . . Yet the cardinals of the Society were expressly obliged to forbid the Jesuits, upon pain of excommunication, to allow the worship of idols under any pretext whatever and to conceal the mystery of the cross from those they instructed in the faith, commanding positively that they admit no one to baptism until after such instruction and enjoining them to exhibit a crucifix in their churches. This is amply detailed in a decree of the congregation dated 9 July 1646 and signed by Cardinal Capponi.

"In this way they have spread themselves all over the world by their doctrine of *probable opinions*, which is the cause and basis of all this disorder. You must learn what it is from their own testimony, for they make no effort to conceal it anymore than they do the facts I am stating. Except they do say they veil their human and political prudence under the pretext of divine and Christian prudence. As if faith, supported by tradition, were not invariable in all times and places. Instead, they will bend the rule to accommodate the person who was to submit to it, as if there were no ways to forgive those with stains of guilt other than by corrupting the law of God itself. But the law of the Lord is perfect, converting the soul by conforming it to its salutary directions!

"So come and visit these worthy Fathers, and you will immediately see the reason for their doctrine respecting grace, in the laxity of their morals. You will see the Christian virtues so disguised and so lacking in love, which is their life and soul, and will see so many crimes palliated and so many disorders permitted, it will no longer appear strange that they should maintain 'that all men have at all times sufficient grace to lead'—in their sense of the phrase—'a religious life.' Since their morality is entirely pagan, nature is sufficient to guide them. When we affirm the need of efficacious grace, the perspective brings other virtues into view. It is not enough to cure vices by other vices and to merely induce men to conform to the external duties of religion. It is to practice a nobler virtue than that of the Pharisees or the sages of the pagan world. Law and reason are sufficient for these effects. But to free the soul from the love of the world, to withdraw it from what is an object of the fondest affection, to enable a man to die to himself and to love God with utter and unalterable attachment, can only be accomplished by an omnipotent power. It is as irrational to pretend we possess a perfect command over these graces as it is to deny that those virtues which do not include the love of God, and which the Jesuits confuse with Christian virtues, are not possible in our own strength."

Until now my friend had spoken with deep concern, for he is much affected by these disorders. For myself, I congratulated the skill of Jesuit policy and went immediately to one of their best casuists, with whom I wanted to renew acquaintance. So knowing how to proceed, I had no difficulty in introducing and conducting the subject. Retaining his attachment to me, I was welcomed by many expressions of kindness, and after some preliminary discussion I took the opportunity to ask about fasting. I mentioned how difficult I found it to practice. He exhorted me to resist my own disinclinations. But when I persisted in my complaints, he became compassionate and began to make excuses on my behalf. Many of those he offered did not fit my taste, until at length he asked if I could not sleep without having had supper.

"No, it's because of that that I am obliged to breakfast at noon and to sup late at night," I said.

"I'm very glad that you have discovered an innocent way of relieving your anxiety. Go on as you are doing, for you have no obligation to fast. However, don't depend on my word, but come with me into the library."

So I went in and he said, taking up a book, "Here is your proof, and O, what a splendid one it is! Provided by Escobar."

"Who is Escobar?"

"What, are you so ignorant of the name of Escobar, of our Society, who has compiled this moral theology from twenty-four of our Fathers, who in his preface compares the book to 'that of the Revelation which was sealed with seven seals,' and says that Jesus delivered it thus sealed to the four living creatures, Suarez, Vasquez, Molina, and Valentia, in the presence of the four and twenty Jesuits, who represent the four and twenty elders? Now see, it says 'He who cannot sleep without his supper, is he obliged to fast? By no means.' Are you now satisfied?"

The good Father, seeing my satisfaction, proceeded ecstatically: "Look here at this passage in Filiutius, one of the four and twenty Jesuits: 'Suppose someone is exhausted, is he obliged to fast? Certainly not. But suppose he has fatigued himself for the purpose of being released from fasting, must he then observe it? No—although it was his premeditated design, he is still not obliged.' Would you ever have believed this?" appealing to me.

"Why, I must be dreaming. Am I really listening to religious talk in this way? Tell me, Father, are you absolutely and conscientiously convinced of all this?"

"No, certainly."

"Then why speak against your own conscience?"

"Not at all: I wasn't speaking according to my conscience but in conformity to the authorities. And you follow them with safety simply because they are skillful polemicists."

"What! Because they have inserted these lines in their writings, am I allowed to search out occasions and pretexts to commit sin? I thought only the Scriptures and the tradition of the church constituted the one rule of conduct, not your casuists!"

In amazement he said, "Why, you remind me absolutely of the Jansenists! Is it not in the power of authorities such as Father Bauny and Basil Pontius to make their opinions probable?"

"But I am not satisfied with probability, I am anxious to know certainty."

"Oh, you know nothing respecting the doctrine of *probable opinions*. If you did, you would speak very differently. You must really come under my instruction. For I can assure you, you haven't wasted time by coming here today. Without being acquainted with this doctrine, you can know nothing. It's the very foundation, the ABC of all our morality," he replied.

Intrigued by this, I asked him to tell me what he meant by a *probable opinion*.

"Our authorities will furnish you with the best explanation," he said. "All of them, including the four and twenty elders, agree on the following principle: 'An opinion is called *probable* when it is founded upon reasons of some importance. So it sometimes happens that only one very serious doctor can render an opinion probable.' See the argument, 'for a man who is particularly devoted to study would not adopt an opinion unless he had a good and sufficient reason for doing so.'"

"And so, can a single doctor turn and overturn, settle and unsettle, the consciences of people at his own pleasure and always be safe?"

"Sir," he said, "you must not ridicule or think of opposing this doctrine. Whenever the Jansenists have tried to do it, they have failed completely. No, no, it is too firmly established."

[Here the Jesuit referred to other authorities.]

"Charming, charming, my good Father; your doctrine is admirably accommodating indeed! To have always a reply ready at hand, yes or no, just as you please; what an inestimable privilege, and how can it be valued enough! Now I see the use which you doctors made of their contrary opinions in all subjects. There is always one for you, and the other is never against you. If you do not find your account in one way, you are sure to do so in another. So you are always safe."

"True, true; if one God distress us, another will defend us."

"But what happens if I have consulted one of your experts and taken his opinion, which left me entirely free, and then find myself caught by a confessor who refuses absolution without making any change of attitude? Have you provided for such an occasion, Father?"

"Certainly, they are obliged to absolve their penitents who hold some *probable opinions*, upon pain of committing a mortal offense. So they can never be at a loss. This is clearly stated by our Fathers, among whom is Father Bauny, who says: 'When the penitent follows a *probable opinion*, the confessor must absolve him, although his opinion is contrary to that of the penitent.' "

"But Father, he does not affirm that it would be a mortal sin not to absolve him."

"How quick you are! Hear how he proceeds to this specific conclusion: 'To refuse to absolve a penitent who acts conformably to a *probable opinion* is a sin in its own nature mortal.' He quotes to confirm this, three of our most distinguished divines, Suarez, Vasquez, and Sanchez."

"O my good Father," I said, "how admirable are all the regulations you have adopted! No excuse remains for future apprehension, for no confessor will ever dare to disobey. But I had no idea of your power to enjoin upon pain of damnation. I imagined you only capable of taking away sins, not thinking that you could introduce them. Now I see you can do everything."

"That is not quite right," he said. "We cannot introduce sins, we can only point them out. I more than once observed that you are not well versed in scholastic theology."

"Be that as it may, Father, but my doubts are thus completely removed. However, I have another question. What do you do when the Fathers of the church are in direct opposition to any one of your casuists?"

"What extraordinary ignorance! The Fathers were a good authority for the morals of their own age, but they lived at a time too remote for us. They can no longer regulate our lives. This belongs to the new casuists. Listen to what some of them have to tell us, such as Father Cellot: 'In questions of morality, the new casuists are preferable to the ancient Fathers, although they lived closer to the apostolic times.' "

I replied, "O what charming maxims, and how full of comfort!"

He replied, "We leave the Fathers to those who treat a *positive* divinity. But we who guide the consciences of men read them but little and quote no writings except those of the new casuists. If you consult Diana you will find that of his list of 296 authors, the oldest is eighty years ago."

"Was this not about the time of the foundation of your Society?"

"Yes, about then."

"Is that to say that as soon as you made your appearance in the world, Augustine, Chrysostom, Ambrose, Jerome, and others were obliged to withdraw? But may I at least be informed of the names of their successors? Who are these new authors?"

[Here the Father mentioned names, none known to this day.]

"Oh my Father," I exclaimed in great alarm, "were all these people really Christians?"

"How do you mean, Christians? Did I not state that by these men alone, we at this moment govern all Christendom?"

I felt very sad, but I couldn't express it, so I contented myself with asking if all these authors were Jesuits.

"No," he replied, "but that is of no importance. But they have all nevertheless written many excellent things. Most of them, indeed, have borrowed from our own authors, or have copied from ours, but we are not scrupulous about that. Besides, they constantly quote and eulogize our authors."

"Now I see it," I commented, "all are acceptable except the ancient Fathers, and so you remain in full possession of the field. You can take any direction you want, and you can wander wherever you like; but I see there are three or four major barriers that will obstruct your progress."

"And pray," asked the Father in amazement, "what are they?"

"The Holy Scriptures, the Popes, and Councils, whom you cannot contradict, and who all agree with the gospel."

"O ho! Is that all? You really frighten me. Do you imagine that so obvious a case as this has not been anticipated and provided for? I am truly amazed that you should think we are opposed to Scripture, to Popes, and to Councils. You shall have clear demonstration to the contrary. I would have been exceedingly upset that you should suppose we are deficient in our duty. But if you return tomorrow I will undertake to furnish you with complete information on this subject, too."

So ended our meeting, and here I close my letter. I flatter myself that you will find enough here to afford you amusement until I write again.

I am, et cetera.

LETTER X
EASY EXPEDIENCE OF THE JESUITS
WITH REGARD TO THE SACRAMENT
OF PENITENCE.
THEIR MAXIMS IN REGARD TO CONFESSION,
ABSOLUTION, CONTRITION,
AND THE LOVE OF GOD

Paris, 2 August 1656

Sir,

I have not yet come to the investigation of the politics of the Society, but I proceed to one of its great principles. You will now have an opportunity to see those allowances with regard to confession which certainly must comprise the very best expedient the Jesuits could have devised to please all and offend none. It was necessary to know this before we go further, so for this reason the Father considered it proper to give me the following instructions:

"You have seen by what I have already described how successfully our Fathers have worked to show by their superior wisdom that many things are now permitted which formerly were forbidden. But as some sins are still indefensible, and the only remedy for them is confession, it is necessary to overcome this difficulty in the way I am about to mention. Having previously shown you how certain conscientious scruples may be removed, by showing that what was once supposed to be sinful is not really so, it only remains for me to point out the way of expiating real sins with ease, by making confession easy when it was formerly so difficult."

"Please Father, how is this accomplished?"

"By those splendid subtleties," he said, "which are peculiar to our Society. It is by these inventions that crimes which are now expiated with tears can be done with more gladness and zeal than they were once committed. Many people can remove their sense of guilt as soon as it is perpetrated."

"O, I ask you Father," I said, "teach me some of these useful ways of doing it."

"Well, sir, there are a considerable number of them. There are many painful things in confession which we have eased up on. The principal difficulties consist in the shame of confessing certain sins, the details with which certain circumstances must be explained, and the way penance must be done. But now I shall try to show you that there is nothing difficult in all this because of the extreme care which has been taken to remove all the unpalatable bitterness out of so essential a remedy.

"I begin with the pain which the confession of some kinds of sin brings. It is often important, as you know, to preserve the esteem of your confessor. So our Fathers, among them Escobar and Suarez, have suggested that you need two confessors, 'one for mortal and the other for venial sins, in order to keep up a good reputation with your ordinary confessor. Provided, of course, that you don't continue in a state of mortal sin.'

"Another ingenious device is this: After confessing to your ordinary confessor, without letting him see that the sin was previously committed since your last confession, give a general confession and include your last sin with the others. For the confessor, except in certain cases which rarely occur, has no right to inquire whether the sin of which the individual accuses himself is habitual. He also has no right to force the individual to confess sins to the shame of divulging his frequent relapses and falls."

"How can this be, Father? It's like saying that a doctor has no right to ask his patient about the time when he was struck with a fever. Do not all sins differ from each other according to the circumstances? Ought not then a genuine penitent disclose to his confessor the whole condition of his conscience, with the same sincerity and openness as if he were speaking to Jesus Christ, whose place is taken by the priest? Is not that person far from having a true disposition if he conceals his frequent relapses in order to veil the seriousness of his transgressions?"

I could see that the good Father was embarrassed. He tried to evade the answer by urging me to consider another of their rules which only showed a new disorder without in the least dealing with the previous.

"I admit," he said, "that habit increases the seriousness of sin, but it does not change its nature. Because of this, the penitent is not obliged to confess according to the law established by our Fathers and cited by Escobar: 'No one is obliged to confess more than the circumstances which changed the nature of his sin, not those which rendered it more odious.'" [Here he cited more.]

"Very convenient, very accommodating devices of devotion indeed!" I said.

"Yes, but all would mean nothing if we did not try to mitigate the severity of penance which is very much opposed to confession. But now the most delicate have nothing to fear, since we have insisted in our theses in the College of Clermont, 'that if the confessor impose a convenient and suitable penance, and yet he should not want to accept it, he can withdraw and renounce both the absolution and penance imposed.'"

"Well then," I observed, "confession should not be called the sacrament of penance."

"There you are wrong," he said. "For it is necessary to enjoin someone at least for the sake of the form."

"But Father, do you think a man deserves absolution when he objects to the least painful service to expiate his offenses? When people have such a state of mind, ought you not rather to retain than remit their sins? Do you have a true view of the nature of your ministry, and are you not aware that you possess the power of binding and loosing? Do you think it is lawful to give absolution indifferently to those who ask it, without previously knowing whether Jesus Christ looses in heaven those whom you loose upon earth?"

"Fine talk indeed, sir! But do you think we are ignorant that 'the confessor is to make himself the judge of the disposition of his penitent, both because he is under an obligation not to dispense the sacraments to those who are unworthy of them, Jesus Christ having commended him to be faithful to his charge, and not to give the children's bread to dogs. Because he is to be a judge, and it is the duty of a judge to judge justly, ought he to absolve those who Jesus Christ condemns?'"

"Please Father, whose words are these?"

"I have been quoting Filiutius."

"You amaze me. I thought they were the words of one of the Fathers of the church. But this passage ought to impress confessors deeply and make them extremely cautious in dispensing the sacrament and so find out whether the sorrow of their penitence is genuine and whether their promises to avoid future transgressions is really true."

"There is no difficulty about that," said the Father. "Filiutius has taken care to avoid any embarrassment to the confessors. So following the words I have cited, he suggests this easy device: 'The confessor may make himself quite easy about the disposition of his penitent. If he does not find sufficient evidence of his grief, the confessor has only to ask if he does not detest sin in his heart. If he says yes, then he is obliged to believe him. The same is true about his future resolution.'"

[Here the Father went on to point out that the confessor may in fact see that the penitent is not truly penitent at all.]

I understood his meaning perfectly. For he had before assured me that the confessor ought to be satisfied simply with a verbal regret. I was now so revolted by all this that I was on the point of breaking off the conversation, but managed to restrain my feelings in order to see it through. So I contented myself with asking, "What agreement is there between this doctrine and that of the gospel, which requires us to pluck out our eyes and forfeit necessities when they are prejudicial to our salvation? How can you imagine that a man who indulges in these occasions of sin can genuinely detest it? Is it not on the contrary too obvious that he is not aware of its enormity, as he should be, and that he is far from that true conversion of heart which would make him love God as much as he had before loved things?"

"How surprisingly you talk!" he said. "That would be true contrition. You don't seem to know that all the Fathers teach unanimously that it is an error, close to heresy, to represent contrition as essential and to maintain that the shallow remorse for sin arising solely from the fear of hell, which keeps someone from sinning openly, is not enough with the sacrament."

"I believe this doctrine is peculiar to your Fathers. For others who believe that mere attrition is sufficient with the sacrament maintain that at least it should be mixed with some love to God. When you say that attrition, arising solely from the fear of punishment, is sufficient with the sacrament for the justification of sinners, does it not follow that a person may expiate his own sins and be saved without ever loving God throughout the whole course of his life? Will your Fathers dare then to maintain this principle?"

"I see by your question that you want to know the doctrine of our Fathers with regard to the love of God. It is the last and most important point in their morality, which you might have seen by the quotations I have mentioned on the subject of contrition. But please do not interrupt me while I am giving others of a more precise nature upon the love of God, for the consequences of these are significant." [Here he cited a number of his authorities.]

I permitted him to continue with this nonsense, which was a surprising display of the arrogance with which the human mind can treat the love of God. [More absurd discussion followed; he concluded with the following.]

"Thus our Fathers have discharged mankind from the painful obligation of actually loving God with all the heart. So profitable is this doctrine that our Fathers have released us from the troublesome obligation of loving God, which is the privilege of the evangelical as distinguished from the Jewish law. One authority says, 'It is reasonable that by the law of grace in the New Testament, God should do away with the irksome and difficult duty which was attached to the rigorous law of exercising an act of complete contrition in order to be justified, and that he should institute sacraments to make up for our defects and to facilitate obedience. Otherwise Christians, who are the children, could not receive the good graces of their Father any more readily than the Jews, who were slaves, and yet who obtained mercy from their God.' "

"O, Father," I burst out, "you make me lose all patience. I am horrified at these statements."

"I am not responsible," he said.

"I know very well they are not your own words," I replied, "but you cite them without any sign of disapproval. In fact, you esteem them highly for having pronounced them. Have you no awareness that your concurrence makes you a partner of their crimes? Can you be so ignorant that the apostle Paul judges worthy of death not only those who originate wickedness but those who consent to it? But you go even further, and the liberty you take to corrupt the most sacred rules of Christian conduct extends even to the entire subversion of the divine laws. You violate the great commandment which contains both the law and the prophets. You stab piety to the very heart. You take away and quench the spirit which gives life. You affirm that the love of God is not necessary to salvation. You even assert that 'this exemption from loving God is a great benefit which Christ has brought to the world.' All this is the very acme and depth of impiety.

"What! The price of the blood of Christ obtains exemption from loving him! Prior to the incarnation man was obliged to love God, but since God so loved the world that he gave his only begotten Son, shall the world thus redeemed be discharged from the duty of loving him? What strange theology we have in our days! You dare to remove the anathema which the apostle Paul pronounces against those who do not love the Lord Jesus Christ. You destroy what the apostle John says, that he that loves not abides in death! Even the declaration of Christ himself you take away: 'He that loves me not keeps not my commandments.' In this way you make those who never once loved God in all their lives worthy of enjoying his presence forever! Surely this is the mystery of iniquity now brought to completion.

"O, my good Father, at last open your eyes. If you are not so completely influenced with the other absurd doctrines of your casuists, let these latter examples undermine your confidence by their sheer extravagance. I wish this for you with all my heart and in all brotherly love, pray God that he would condescend to show you how false and dangerous is such teaching. Instead may he fill with his love the hearts of those who dare to dispense others from this obligation."

After further discourse of this kind, I left the Jesuit. It is scarcely likely that I shall visit him again. It need not, however, cause you any regret. For if it was necessary to explain any more of their maxims, I have now read enough of their writings to be able to tell you almost as much of their morality, and perhaps more of their politics, than he has already done.

I am, et cetera.

A Prayer of Pascal,
Asking God to Use Sickness in His Life
Appropriately

1. O Lord, whose Spirit is so good and gracious in all things, and who is so merciful that not only prosperities but even the adversities that happen to your elect are the effects of your mercy, give me grace not to act like the unbelievers in the state you bring me into by your justice. Instead, like a true Christian, help me to acknowledge you as my Father and my God, in whatever circumstances you may place me. For no change of my circumstances can ever alter your will for my life. You are ever the same, though I may be subject to change. You are no less God when you are afflicting and punishing me than when you are consoling and showing compassion.

2. You gave me health to use in your service, but I misused it to a wholly secular use. Now you have sent me a sickness for my correction. O let me not use this likewise to provoke you, by my impatience. I abused my health, and you have rightly dealt with me. O keep me now from abusing that also. And since the corruption of my nature distorts your favors to me, grant, O my God, that your all-prevailing grace may render your chastenings to be beneficial. If my heart has been in love with the world when I was in robust health, destroy my vigor to promote my salvation. Whether it be by weakness of

body or by zeal for your love, render me incapable of enjoying the worldly idols, that my delight may be only in you.

3. O God, to whom I must render an exact account of all my actions at the end of my life and at the end of the world, help me to prepare now for this end. O God, who allows the world and all the events to happen within it for the trial of your elect and for the punishment of the wicked, keep these realities within my soul. . . . Help me to anticipate the awful day of judgment by already destroying everything that would keep me from thinking of these things to come. If you do this by giving me ill health so that I am prevented from enjoying the ways of the world, I can only thank you for doing so. If this is how you destroy the idols that would keep me from you, I can only give you thanks. . . . For one day, I shall be stripped of everything, when I appear before your judgment, standing alone before your Presence, to answer to your justice for all the attitudes of my heart. . . . Grant then that I may so anticipate my death that I may find mercy hereafter in your sight.

4. Grant, O Lord, that I may in silence adore all the order of your wonderful providence in the disposal of my life. May your rod comfort me. Having lived in the bitterness of my sins while I was in health, may I now taste the heavenly sweetness of your grace through these afflictions that you have imposed upon me. But I confess, O my God, that my heart is so hardened, so full of worldly ideas, cares, anxieties, and attachments, that neither health nor sickness, neither talks, nor books, not even your holy Scriptures, nor the gospel, nor your most holy mysteries, can do anything at all to bring about my conversion. Certainly it cannot be philanthropy, fastings, miracles, the sacraments, nor all my efforts, nor even those of all the world put together, that can do this. It is only the amazing greatness of your grace that can do this.

So I look up to you, O my God, you who are Almighty God, to give me this gift that all creatures together could never give. Yet I would not dare to direct my cries to you, were it not that no one else could ever hear them except you. But, O my God, the conversion of my heart, which I ask of you, is a work that exceeds all the powers of nature. So I can only ask of you, Almighty Author and Master of nature. For everything that is not God is unable to fulfill my desires. It is you alone I seek, that I may have you. O Lord, open my heart. Enter into this rebellious place that my sins have possessed. For they hold it in subjection. Do enter in, as into the strong man's house. But first bind the strong and powerful enemy, who is tyrant over it. Take to yourself the treasures that are there. Lord, take my affections which the world has robbed me of; spoil the world of this treasure. Rather, continue to possess it, for it belongs only to you. It is a tribute I owe you, for all belongs to you, for your own image is stamped upon it. You put it there at the moment of my baptism, which was my second birth. But now it is wholly defaced. The image of the world is so strongly engraved upon it that your own image is no longer discernible. Yet you who alone could create my soul, you alone can create it anew. You alone could create it in your image, so you alone can reproduce it, and reimpress that defaced image. Jesus Christ, my Savior, the express image and character of your essence is that image and likeness I desire.

5.   O my God, how happy is the heart that can love so wonderful an object, where the affection is so glorious and the attachment so beneficial! I feel I cannot love the world without displeasing you or without hurting and dishonoring myself. Yet the world is still the object of my delight. O my God, how happy are the souls whose delight is only in you. For they give themselves wholly up to loving you. They do this without scruple of conscience, so how firm and lasting is their happiness! Their expectation can never be frustrated. Since you never fail, neither life nor death can ever separate them from the object of their desires. The very moment which shall involve the wicked, with their idols, in one common ruin, shall unite the just to you in one common

glory. . . . So how happy are those who with complete freedom and invincible inclination of their will love perfectly and freely what they are necessarily under obligation to love.

6. Perfect are the good desires you have given me. Be their End, as you have been their Beginning. Crown your own gifts, for I recognize they are your gifts. Instead of presuming that it is by my prayers that I have them, rather I acknowledge they are solely of your grace. For I have nothing in myself that could oblige you to give to me. Indeed, all the moments of my heart are directed only toward creaturely things, or else toward myself, and they only provoke you. So I thank you, O my God, for the good desires you have inspired. Help me to thank you for them.

7. Touch my heart with repentance for my faults. Because without this inward pain, the outward evils with which you have afflicted my body will be a new occasion of sin . . . so let my sickness be the remedy itself by making me consider from the pains I feel, those which I am morally insensitive to feel, for my soul is diseased and insensitive. O Lord, the greatest of my maladies is indeed this insensibility to sin and all its weaknesses. Make me to feel them deeply, and grant that the rest of my life will be one continued penitence, to wash away the sins I have committed.

8. O Lord, although my past life has been kept from grievous crimes, yet I have done things exceedingly hateful to you. For I have had constant negligence of your Word, in contempt of its divine inspiration. I have misused the holy sacraments. So the idleness of my life has been wholly unprofitable in actions, thoughts, and a complete waste of all the time you have given me in which to worship you. Instead of serving your business, I have served my own business, not serving your pleasure. I have not been penitent for my daily trespasses, so that my life has not been one of daily repentance as it should have been. I have failed in the practice of a righteous life before you.

9.   Thus, O God, I have always been a rebel against you. Yes, Lord, I have always been deaf to your inspirations. I have despised your oracles. I have judged contrary to what you judge. I have contradicted those holy truths you brought into the world from the bosom of your Eternal Father, and according to which you will judge the world. . . . Yea, Lord, I confess that I esteemed health as a good, not because it is a means of serving you, but because with it I could exercise less restraints and self-discipline to enjoy the things of this life and to better relish its fatal pleasures. Grant me the grace to rectify my reason and conform my feelings to your ways. So may I account myself happy in affliction, so that while I am incapable of external actions, you may so purify my thoughts that they may no longer contradict your own. Thus may I find you within myself, while my bodily weakness incapacitates me from seeking you without. For, O Lord, your kingdom is in the hearts of the faithful. I shall find it in myself if I discover there your Spirit and your Wisdom.

10.   But what shall I do, O Lord, to engage you to pour down your Spirit on this miserable clay? For I am odious in your sight. Nor can I find anything in myself that can be acceptable to you. I am nothing, O Lord, but my sufferings alone, which have some resemblance to yours. Look down therefore on the evils I struggle with which threaten me. Look with the eye of mercy on the wounds your hand has made. O God, who became incarnate after the fall of man and did take on a body to suffer all the penalty of sin for us with that body—you, O God, who suffered for us in that body, accept my body. Not for its own sake, nor for all that it contains, for all deserves your wrath, but on account of the sufferings it endures, which alone can be worthy of your love. May my sufferings invite you to visit me.

To complete the preparation of your stay, grant, O my Savior, that if my body has this in common with yours, that it suffers for my offenses, may my soul have likewise in common with your soul to be sorrowful for those offenses. Thus may I suffer with you and like you, both in my body and in my soul, for the transgressions I have committed.

11. Grant me, O Lord, grace to join your consolations to my sufferings, that I may suffer like a Christian. I pray not to be exempted from pain, for this is the recompense of saints. But I pray that I may not be abandoned to the pains of nature without the comforts of your Spirit. For this is the cure of those who know you not. I pray not to enjoy fullness of comfort without suffering, for that is the life of glory. Neither do I pray for fullness of suffering without comfort, for that is the state of the Jews. But I pray, O Lord, that I may feel at once both the pains of nature for my sins and the consolations of your Spirit by your grace; for that is the true state of the Christian. O, may I never feel pain without comfort! But may I feel pain and consolation together, that I may afterwards attain to feel only your comforts without any mixture of pain! For you did leave the world to languish in natural sufferings without consolation, until the coming of your only Son. But now, you console and sweeten the sufferings of your faithful servants by the grace of your only Son, and fill your saints with pure joy in the glory of your only Son. These are the wonderful steps by which you have carried on your works. You have raised me from the first. O, lead me to the second, so that I may attain the third! O Lord, this mercy I earnestly implore.

12. Suffer me not, O Lord, to be so estranged from you that I cannot reflect upon your soul being sorrowful, even unto death, and your body overcome by death on my account, without rejoicing to suffer with you in my own body and in my soul. For what could be more shameful than for Christians to gratify the flesh, while our Lord is left to suffer on our behalf? By baptism we have renounced the world to become your disciples. We have pledged ourselves to live and die for you. . . . To seek pleasures in such fashion in the light of these truths, and others also, is criminal indeed. So it was most just, O Lord, you should interrupt so wrong a joy as this kind of life. This comforts me while even living in the shadow of death.

13. Therefore take from me, O Lord, that self-pity which love of myself so readily produces, and from the frustration of not succeeding in the world as I would naturally desire, for these have no regard for your glory. Rather, create in me a sorrow that is conformable to your own. Let my pains rather express the happy condition of my conversion and salvation. Let me no longer wish for health or life, but to spend it and end it for you, with you, and in you. I pray neither for health nor sickness, life nor death. Rather I pray that you will dispose of my health, my sickness, my life, and my death, as for your glory, for my salvation, for the usefulness to your church and your saints, among whom I hope to be numbered. You alone know what is expedient for me. You are the Sovereign Master. Do whatever pleases you. Give me or take away from me. Conform my will to yours, and grant that with a humble and perfect submission, and in holy confidence, I may dispose myself utterly to you. May I receive the orders of your everlasting, provident care. May I equally adore whatever proceeds from you.

14. With perfect consistency of mind, help me to receive all manner of events. For we know not what to ask, and we cannot ask for one event rather than another without presumption. We cannot desire a specific action without presuming to be a judge, and assuming responsibility for what in your wisdom you may hide from me. O Lord, I know only one thing, and that is that it is good to follow you and wicked to offend you. Beyond this, I do not know what is good for me, whether health or sickness, riches or poverty, or anything else in this world. This knowledge surpasses both the wisdom of men and of angels. It lies hidden in the secrets of your providence, which I adore, and will not dare to pry open.

15. Grant, O Lord, that being what I am, I may conform myself to your will. Being as sick as I am now, may I glorify you in my sufferings. Without these I cannot attain to your glory. For you, O Lord, O my Savior, likewise did not please to attain except through sufferings. It was by the marks of

your sufferings that you were made known again to your disciples, and it is by the sufferings that they endure that you also make yourself known to your disciples still. Own me as your disciple in the afflictions which I endure, in my body and in my mind, for the sins I have committed. And as nothing is acceptable to God unless presented by you, unite my will to yours and my sufferings to those you have endured. Unite me to yourself, fill me with yourself, and with your Holy Spirit. Enter my heart and into my soul. There, sustain my afflictions, and continue to endure there in me what remains of your passion. For you fulfill in your members until the perfect consummation of your mystical Body, so that being filled by you, it may no longer be I who lives or suffers, but you, O my Savior, who lives and suffers in me. Having thus become a small partaker of your sufferings, may you fill me completely with that glory you have acquired by them and in which you live, with the Father and the Holy Spirit, for ever and ever, AMEN.

Scripture Index

Subject Index

(Numbers in parentheses indicate numbering for this edition of the *Pensées*. All other numbers are page numbers.)